Designers' Own Homes

ARCHITECTURAL DIGEST

Designers' Own Homes

EDITED BY PAIGE RENSE
Editor-in-chief, *Architectural Digest*

The Knapp Press   Publishers   Los Angeles

Published by The Knapp Press
5900 Wilshire Boulevard, Los Angeles, California 90036

LIBRARY OF CONGRESS CATALOGING IN PUBLICATION DATA
Main entry under title:

Designers' own homes.

1. Interior decorators—Homes and haunts—United States. 2. Interior decoration—United States—History—20th century. I. Rense, Paige. II. Architectural digest.
NK2115.3.157D4   1984   728'.092'2   84-12188
ISBN 0-89535-141-2

Printed and bound in the United States of America

"*Could we teach taste or genius by rules,*
they would be no longer taste and genius."

Sir Joshua Reynolds
Discourses on Art
December 14, 1770

Contents

Foreword by PAIGE RENSE *ix*

Introduction by RUSSELL LYNES *xi*

KALEF ALATON *2*
BEVERLY HILLS

VAL ARNOLD *10*
HOLLYWOOD

JOSEPH BRASWELL *18*
MANHATTAN

ROBERT BRAY/MICHAEL SCHAIBLE *26*
MANHATTAN

ELEANOR BROWN *34*
SOUTHAMPTON

DIANE BURN *42*
SAN FRANCISCO

STEVE CHASE *50*
RANCHO MIRAGE

LEO DENNIS/JERRY LEEN *58*
LOS ANGELES

MICHAEL DE SANTIS *66*
MANHATTAN

RUBÉN DE SAAVEDRA *74*
NEW YORK

ANGELO DONGHIA *82*
KEY WEST

TED GRABER *90*
WEST LOS ANGELES

BRUCE GREGGA *98*
LOS ANGELES

ALBERT HADLEY *106*
MANHATTAN

ANTHONY HAIL *114*
SAN FRANCISCO

KEITH IRVINE *122*
NEW ENGLAND

SALLY SIRKIN LEWIS *130*
BEVERLY HILLS

LOYD RAY TAYLOR/CHARLES PAXTON GREMILLION, JR. *138*
DALLAS

ANTHONY MACHADO *146*
SAN FRANCISCO

ROBERT METZGER *155*
MANHATTAN

JOSEPH MINTON/DAVID CORLEY *162*
FORT WORTH

LEE RADZIWILL *170*
MANHATTAN

VALERIAN RYBAR *178*
NEW YORK

JAY SPECTRE *186*
MANHATTAN

LEONARD STANLEY *194*
LOS ANGELES

MICHAEL TAYLOR *202*
SAN FRANCISCO

Credits 211

Foreword

Paige Rense

A designer's own home is like an artist's self-portrait: colored by old dreams and new concepts, with judicious brushstrokes of a disciplined professionalism.

"It's extremely difficult," Jay Spectre concedes, "to draw the line between my privacy and what I want the public to perceive about me."

Basically, designers doing their own homes are indulging in that most delightful of all pastimes, pleasing themselves—a luxury not always feasible in their professional pursuits.

Architects in Victorian days used to rely on an omnipresent expert known as Clerk of the Works. For an interior designer, designing his or her own home is being clerk of the works in its most exhilarating sense.

Everyone has, I think, in some quiet corner of the mind, an ideal home waiting to become a reality. Edgar Allan Poe is not a name that springs lightly to mind in a discussion of interior design, yet even the author of "*The Murders in the Rue Morgue*" and "The Raven" had an ideal home in his thoughts. In "Philosophy of Furniture," appearing in *Gentleman's Magazine* in 1840, he described the "internal decoration" of his ideal living room: "A small and not ostentatious chamber some thirty feet in length and twenty-five in breadth," with window panes "of a crimson-tinted glass" and "curtains of an exceedingly rich crimson silk, fringed with a deep network of gold, and lined with . . . silver tissue. *Repose* speaks in all," said Mr. Poe, summing it up, and he sternly criticized the display of wealth, contending that "as we grow rich, our ideas grow rusty."

The designers whose homes are shown in this book are rich in talent, and their ideas are far from rusty. As the interiors reveal, these gifted men and women have reached the pinnacle of their profession primarily because of an innate sense of style. The homes they have designed for themselves are completely individual statements, unrestricted by the needs of others.

"It's essential for me to live with beautiful things," Michael Taylor says of his home. "Nothing is a prop, and nothing here is simply for effect or acquisition."

To Lee Radziwill, her penthouse represents "the opening up of my life to clarity and simplicity."

"I like space to be pared down," Michael Schaible remarks of his loft apartment, and his partner, Robert Bray, says of his own home, "I think of this space as extremely personal."

That's the common denominator of the uncommon homes in this book: They are all extremely personal. They say what their designers intended them to say: "Tranquillity." "Fun." "Solitude." "Elegance."

But mostly, of course, they say, "Mine!"

PAIGE RENSE

Introduction

As I looked through the handsome photographs and read the articles that have been gathered in this book, I invited them to define for me a style about which I could say, "This is the taste of the seventies and eighties." These interiors say a great deal about recent taste, though not about tastes that everyone shares—even if everyone could afford the kinds of design convictions, impulses, talents and yearnings that are exhibited here. They do not define one style, and that in itself says something revealing about the seventies and eighties.

The photographs turn my mind back to the parlors of Victorian houses and to the drawing rooms of the Edwardians, to opulent interiors occupied by ladies in bustles and gentlemen in frock coats and to the next generation of ladies with pompadours and wasp waists and gentlemen in white flannel, blazers and boaters. Here is what has been called "Victorian clutter" and Edwardian "suitability," so aptly prized by Edith Wharton and Elsie de Wolfe. There are only a few hints of "modern functionalism," though there is its more capricious cousin, Art Déco.

Somehow neither the Victorians nor the Edwardians would be at home in these rooms. There is no reason why they should be and every reason why they shouldn't. After all, their codes of manners were very different from ours, more formal and more what is today called "sexist," a word that Victorian ladies would have thought had vulgar overtones. Edwardian ladies might merely have been offended by a violation of the language; no such word existed in their dictionaries, much less in their conversation. (Indeed,

they would not have known whether *sexist* applied to the exploitation of women by men or the other way around.) These rooms are not ones in which a lady is required, as Victorian and Edwardian ladies were, to sit bolt upright as etiquette demanded with "the base of the spine at the back of the chair," nor are they rooms of the sort in which no lady ever lifted her hands above her shoulders once her hair was coiffured and her face lightly touched with rouge and powder in the privacy of her boudoir.

Yet in many of these interiors, there is a sense of Edwardian formality and elegance, and in others, there is a Victorian delight in bibelots and curios—as reminders of travel, things picked up in strange places, were called—because they were entertaining or tokens of reminiscence or sentiment, or objects intrinsically "beautiful." In other words, they are rooms lovingly assembled as well as expertly designed to be lived in by late-twentieth-century men and women.

They are, however, giveaways.

"Much of the character of every man can be read in his house," wrote Andrew Jackson Downing, the eminent American tastemaker of the first half of the last century. It might be amusing to take these rooms one by one and read them like the palms of hands or like tea leaves, and from the things in them—the furniture and curtains and pictures and books, the miscellany of cherished "found" objects and sentimental ones—read the character of the men and women who designed them for their private purposes. It might be fun, but that is not the purpose of this book. Rather,

Designers' Own Homes

this book reveals to its readers how distinguished designers approach the spaces in which they have chosen to live, what they do to make them handsome, workable, inviting, comfortable and hospitable. This book offers more than that, however.

It is a gallery of handsome furniture, some modern, much from the eighteenth and nineteenth century, some from what, before jets, were considered exotic lands. It is a catalogue of beautiful textiles and ingenious ways to use them; of glass as elaborate as crystal chandeliers and sconces and as straightforward as wineglasses; of rugs as abstract as the canvases of expressionists; of primitive and sophisticated sculpture; of paintings and drawings, prints and mirrors. But unlike a gallery or a catalogue, it is, if you wish it to be, a textbook of how to marry the seemingly irreconcilable, how to achieve a sense of unity out of disparate objects. In some cases, it is a guide to how to create and control happy disorder in a world all too subject to functional solutions achieved by pushing keys on computers. In other words, it is a *sophisticated primer* of how to make formal or informal order without creating sterility.

Europeans have a way of criticizing American taste for its supposed deadly uniformity. Everything, they say, looks the same, and everybody lives alike in Boston and Seattle, in Chicago and Los Angeles. Everywhere, they suggest, is essentially like everywhere else, because the taste of our consumer society is mass-produced, and the assimilation is not just that of looks but in the accents in which we speak, in what we listen to, and in what assaults our eyes. Our taste is homogenized by television. If you should hear a visitor from abroad pronounce such clichés (and you are likely to), hand him or her a copy of this book.

If anyone can draw a diagram of American taste from the illustrations and the comments in this volume, it will be as quixotic as an animated weather map. Taste is like the weather; the winds that condition it blow now from one place, now from another, sometimes benign, sometimes outrageous. Like the weather, everyone talks about taste, but unlike the weather, there are people who do something about it. The men and women whose houses and apartments are illustrated in this volume are in the business of doing just that. Some of their solutions I find congenial to my taste, some I do not. Some you will admire, some you will not, but I can assure you that you'll not be indifferent to any of them, and that each one will instruct you visually and inform you socially.

Downing's contemporary O. S. Fowler, who was a crusader for octagonal houses as the solution to man's domestic and moral problems, made a sententious but not entirely inappropriate remark about the taste of Americans in his day: "Beautiful birds build tasty nests," he wrote; ". . . as a general rule, a fancy man will build a fancy cottage, a practical man a convenient house, a substantial man a solid edifice, a weak man an illy arranged home, an aspiring man a high house, and a superior man a superb villa."

You will agree, I think, that this is a book of consummately tasty nests.

—*Russell Lynes*

Kalef Alaton

"I collect very slowly. I choose something for its shape and scale, rather than for its rarity."

"Istanbul is the land of dreams," says interior designer Kalef Alaton, in a voice as warm as Turkish sunshine. "It is architecturally superb. Everyone has been there—the Greeks, the Ottomans." Surely Mr. Alaton carries his cosmopolitan heritage and an aura of Eastern mystery with him wherever he goes, and his design sense couples an affinity for the exotic with a firm comprehension of the functional.

Until 1983, when he began decorating a new apartment for himself in Los Angeles, Mr. Alaton lived in an apartment in a Beverly Hills townhouse. When he moved there, in 1979, he found himself called upon to do a good deal of interior renovation. While he can frequently second-guess a client's needs, he had difficulty deciding what to do with his own residence. To begin with, there was very little to work with—merely good space, some charm and a lot of cobwebs. "I couldn't make up my mind," he confesses. "It is very difficult when you design for yourself."

His mood lightened considerably once the first major decision was reached—and khaki chosen as the dominant color. Used throughout except in the bedroom and library, it covered walls and furniture, balancing out and creating a base of tranquillity against which other colors could bloom. The color was mixed and given to the dyer, who dyed 250 yards of canvas with it. Everything was done in the same fabric. Nuance became far more important than marked grandeur.

In fact, the living room furniture consisted of only five chairs, but they were the perfect size for comfort and easily movable for pleasant conversation. Judiciously placed and skillfully lighted artworks provided the necessary touches of romance and intrigue. Two figures from a church in Liège floated against the plain khaki walls. Jars and vases used in the living room were very old— a few from Syria, one Phoenician example dating from 900 B.C. They were so radiant with history that their spirit dominated the room. In their classic simplicity they proved endlessly seductive, and were arranged together for that very reason.

"I buy things I like," Kalef Alaton says, "and I don't feel the need to have a sample of everything." The only things Mr. Alaton is fiercely possessive of are the books he's acquired; he could not part with any of them, he declares. Perhaps this intensity explains why the library of the Beverly Hills apartment represented a departure in mood and intention from the rest of the interior. Among the rooms, it alone came close to being crowded; it was a cozy hideaway where books provided varied colors, and red drapery a large slash of brightness.

Mr. Alaton frequently used the apartment for entertaining, and those who experienced the rooms at night became part of the tapestry. He remarks that "it was very pleasant at night, with candles and flowers and people. Everything is so much more focused when there are few distractions. The apartment was very relaxing but very austere. For me, it had a wonderful atmosphere." In such surroundings it seemed quite natural to forget that Beverly Hills was just outside, and to imagine the wonders of the East instead. The possibilities seemed many and exotic, for Kalef Alaton succeeded in creating a setting that is simple yet echoes a cosmopolitan sensibility.

"It was very pleasant at night, with candles and flowers and people. Everything is so much more focused when there are few distractions."

ABOVE: Canvas-covered walls and seating contribute a warm, cohesive background in the living room, as in much of the interior. Two 16th-century cherubs hover within ethereal arches of light, embodying the transcendental aura of the décor. On a 17th-century Spanish table, a still life arrangement of Roman, Phoenician and Cypriot pottery introduces arresting shapes and a flavor of antiquity.

OPPOSITE: On a landing leading to the living room, a contemporary painting by Alexius Sotos is intriguingly juxtaposed with a graceful 18th-century marble sculpture.

FOLLOWING PAGES: The living room's light-toned fireplace, flanked by 17th-century Japanese ceremonial spears, enlivens the elegantly subdued palette. Poised upon the dark, gleaming floors are, at left, a 17th-century Persian jar and, at right, an 18th-century French grain vessel. The doorway admits a partial view of Pietro Liberi's Heracles and Omphale.

ABOVE: *An Eastern influence is evident in the dining room, where Russian and Greek icons evoke the splendors of Byzantium. Joining with Louis XIII–style chairs and a large Chinese porcelain vase, they establish the cultural scope and balance of the ensemble.*

OPPOSITE: *High-contrast purity prevails in the master bedroom, where a light-toned ceiling and pleated bed draperies create an uplifting foil for dark oak flooring and lacquered walls. Surmounted by a sinuous jaguar, an Art Déco clock adds a note of exotic mystery. The Minimalist painting by Los Angeles artist Eleanore Lazarof is, like the room itself, a starkly composed space of subtle harmony.*

Val Arnold

*"I saw this house as a transition
to what I'm eventually
going to achieve."*

When interior designer Val Arnold acquired the house in the Outpost Estates, above Hollywood, where he lived until 1982, it was a childhood fantasy come true. "My family moved to Hollywood in 1945, during World War II," he recalls, "and as a boy I worked at a men's clothing store there. The owner of the shop lived in the Outpost Estates—the Bel Air of its time—and it made quite an impression on me. I told myself that *someday* I would be able to live there too."

The initial condition of the house, however, did not live up to Mr. Arnold's fantasies. "Quite simply, it was a shambles. The yard was so overgrown and littered that the pure Hollywood Art Déco design of the house was obscured. The previous owners had painted it a brilliant blue with white trim. There was a sauna by the pool, resembling a dilapidated lean-to, and the interior was really wretched. Friends tried to discourage me from buying the house, telling me it was dark, ugly and oppressive. And no wonder. There were three rows of draperies at every window, and the shrubbery outside blocked the light as well. Very late one night I tore down all the draperies. And then I had every bush and tree torn out, with the exception of the palms. Suddenly you could *see* the house. Suddenly it began to make sense."

Rather than redo the house entirely, Mr. Arnold decided to retain the integrity with which it had been built in 1938 and restore it to its original Art Déco style. "I wanted to bring the house back to Hollywood in a completely first-class manner." What he considers to be the two most important features of the house are found in the entrance hall—a tremendous five-thousand-prism chandelier and an etched-glass staircase. The staircase had been rebuilt seven times before the original owner was pleased. And Val Arnold himself had to have the chandelier reconstructed when it fell and shattered soon after he moved in. To retain the dramatic effect of these two elements of the entrance hall, he added only a Jean-Michel Frank console table and Italian Regency mirrors.

The slightly bowed floor-to-ceiling windows in the living room originally had a door on one side, leading onto a large terrace with a splendid view of Hollywood. The door itself was converted into an extension of the window, and a new entrance to the terrace was made of a corner window with glass doors designed to slide into the wall on each side. Structural changes completed, the designer began to add a few favorite pieces as focal points. "The architecture was so strong, so simple, that there was no need for any tricky decorating," Mr. Arnold explains.

In the living room he placed three Art Déco panels depicting Eskimo hunting scenes, which once hung in the historic Oviatt Building in downtown Los Angeles. He added forest green chairs reproduced from originals in the first-class lounge of the *Queen Mary,* a glass-paneled fireplace screen that echoed the staircase in the entrance hall, and a grand piano—"A very Art Déco touch," says Mr. Arnold. In the dining room there was a copy of a Deskey-designed table from Radio City Music Hall.

Mr. Arnold kept lighting as simple as the lines of the house itself. "I was getting bored with overlighted environments," he says. "To live in a house with elaborate lighting, the client has to have an engineering degree to make it work."

The theme of the house was continued outside, with a garden designed all in white and green. At the front of the house white azaleas were planted; in the back, gardenias, calla lilies, lilies of the Nile and other white flowers. Mr. Arnold explains that the Outpost residence was a fulfillment of one of his fantasies. He is now redecorating his present home—and in the process continuing to realize still other dreams.

*"The architecture was so strong
that there was no need for any
tricky decorating."*

*ABOVE: Visible beyond the living room, the stair rail in
the entrance hall—glass panels etched with light lines—
represents a Hollywood interpretation of Art Déco.*

*RIGHT: In the living room, a hearthside grouping includes
commodious seating and a gleaming Art Déco vase. The
octagonal mirror, floor lamp and the fire screen contribute
quietly distinctive accents. Conceived for the 1925 Paris
Exposition, the hunt scene by Georges Artemoff is one of
three hand-carved wooden panels that originally graced the
historic Oviatt Building in Los Angeles.*

12

Angled walls form an architectural frame for a shimmering
view of Hollywood lights beyond the living room terrace. At
right appears another of Artemoff's mahogany carvings.
The Chinese chair adds an exotic note.

14

A Barry Campion painting seems suspended in lyrical flux beneath the dining room's foil-covered ceiling. Topping the streamlined table and a console are Michael Steiner's geometric sculpture and a formidable Cambodian dog.

In the master bedroom, subtle-hued walls and carpeting
accentuate pristine cotton coverings on the brass bed and
a pair of antique Japanese panels with floral detailing.
Nearby, lacquered tables amplify the Oriental theme. In a
windowed alcove, luxuriant flowers and a Lucite lamp pre-
face the spectacle of the glittering city.

*Moonlight lends the perfect tenor to the brick-paved terrace,
where the designer reproduced an archetype of romantic
Hollywood. Reflections create an illusion in the azure pool.
Even the city—a dance of distant sparkles—plays its part.*

Joseph Braswell

"It's been my nature to move on, to tire of a place almost as soon as it is perfected, always trying to invent a little better wheel."

Three hundred feet above the streets of Manhattan, interior designer Joseph Braswell fairly glows with contentment as he describes life in his Sutton Place apartment. "I think I'll be living here for a good long time," he predicts. "This smallish apartment has everything I need. It's a haven: compact, serene." Mr. Braswell found safe harbor a decade ago in the fifty-story high-rise building that remains his current address, but it took him nearly two years to achieve his halcyon state. For six months he lived with nothing more than a bed and a table, but he happily traded his Spartan discomforts for the opportunity to think unhurriedly about how to meet a provocative challenge.

At the center of his developing plan was the spectacular vista that had drawn him to the building in the first place, a panorama that includes the delicate cat's cradle of the Queensboro Bridge and the busy East River. With the view as a starting point, he decided to design an interior with a contemporary feeling. The building was modern, and as he did not own the apartment, Mr. Braswell chose not to make any major alterations that would one day have to be undone in case he should move. Therefore, he installed track lighting everywhere and designed an integrated system of cabinets and bookshelves, which, while appearing architectural in their massiveness, are in fact freestanding. "Ordinarily I would drop the ceiling and put in recessed lighting," he says; "but here, with a concrete slab overhead, the only workable solution was track lighting. It's perfectly flexible, and with a mixture of floods and spots and dimmers, I can change both quality and quantity of light almost instantly—even while guests are on their way up in the elevators."

The play of noncolors in furniture leads the designer to discuss his personal philosophy of color and texture. "In my work, I am steeped in strong patterns and colors all day, and it's easy to become surfeited. Here at home I wanted to restore myself with a tranquil palette of earth tones." The goal has been achieved and the interior gently animated with a series of complementary textures. The floors are a wall-to-wall expanse of rough-textured, sand-colored sisal, while much of his furniture is in either a flawless lacquer of his own devising or in chrome. Soft, sensuous suede, silky leather, wholesome hopsacking, and brittle, bright mirror further the interplay of textures. As well orchestrated as everything is, Mr. Braswell left himself a generous margin for eccentricity. "Little by little," he says with amusement, "odd touches inevitably crept in to soften my original futuristic intentions—an interesting Chinese table here, a witty Art Déco table and a sunburst of Lucite lighting in the foyer, a couple of English bergères 'in the French manner.' "

In truth, the designer's apartment, for all its crisp modern elements, is a repository for some wonderful curios that reflect his deep interest in tradition, particularly that of the eighteenth century. Certainly the grandest of these in size is the six-foot-high wooden cabinet that dominates one end of the living room. It is a puzzle of drawers and doors designed for architectural tools.

Of quite different character are the starkly beautiful clay masks—ceremonial objects for Balinese ritual—that become the focus of another wall. Mr. Braswell provided the place for them, a barely discernible metal strip that forms the seam between two panels of mirror, before he had any notion of what to display there. As he frequently tells clients when he temporarily leaves undecided some element of a room, "When the right thing comes along, you'll know it." As it turned out, he found the right thing while strolling through the shopping arcade of the United Nations headquarters. The unpainted terra-cotta masks now add yet another handsome and interesting texture to this very personal design for living.

"This smallish apartment has everything I need. It's a haven: compact and serene."

ABOVE: The living room uses large furnishings, geometric lines and smooth surfaces. Carpeting is sisal cording.

OPPOSITE: Designed specifically for the living room is an integrated wall system, desk/dining table and modular seating units based upon ash verticals and lacquered horizontals. The paper sculpture, seen in reflection, is by Nancy Miller. Beyond the draperies is the entrance hall, where a 1930s palm frond console created by Serge Roche for Emilio Terry parts the shirred drapery wall treatment.

The spectacular view was the lure that drew the designer halfway up the fifty-story building. The understated design does not distract from the panoramic vista. The all-glass sitting area of the living room is at once intimate and expansive. The 18th-century chairs are covered in suede.

ABOVE: A 19th-century English folding ladder is pressed into service in the library area of the living room. The convex mirror mounted in the corner reflects the adjoining section of the L-shaped room.

OPPOSITE: The bedroom continues the restful atmosphere. Handcrafted ash louver doors exemplify the meticulous detailing throughout; the mirrored headboard wall reflects an 18th-century architect's cabinet in the living room.

Robert Bray   Michael Schaible

"Socially I'm very active
and involved with other
people—but not here at
home. I think of this space
as extremely personal—a
hideout—like the tree
house I had as a boy in
Texas."

"I like space to be pared
down. I have very few
things, and those I keep
in the bookcase."

In search of new directions and interesting effects, a number of interior designers have for the past several years been using decorative elements closely allied to the industrial world. Consequently, in many contemporary homes, familiar objects are turning up, serving purposes for which they were not originally intended. Gymnasium lockers, mover's pads, subway grating, glass bricks, hospital sinks—there seems to be little, in fact, that cannot be put to use by imaginative interior designers. This discovery of industrial objects adds a new dimension to the practice of design today.

Many of the new directions and interesting effects can be found in the work of Bray-Schaible, one of America's forward-looking young interior design partnerships. The team's well-mannered interiors have become known for their sobriety and high level of elegance. The two designers manage to employ an extensive vocabulary of industrial items that at one time would have been considered most unorthodox in residential interiors: restaurant doors, aluminum tambour shades, tables made from restaurant pedestals, tread plate, Colorlith, theatrical spots, factory shelving, concrete accessories and charcoal gray "contract" carpeting. All of this material is edited from the world of industry with a sharp eye for the quality of design as well as for utility. In today's world of declining craftsmanship, many of these products exhibit convincing advances over their more domestic counterparts.

Sitting in his serene downtown Manhattan loft apartment—furnished with black channel-quilted mattresses on industrial-carpet-covered platforms, with office files as nightstands, and restaurant pedestal tables—Michael Schaible declines to discuss High-Tech, a term that he finds tedious because of its overuse. For the designer, qualities that remain exciting beyond the reaches of simple faddishness are the composed elegance and functionalism of the best product design.

His selectiveness is evident in the spareness of his apartment. "I'm not interested in paintings and artworks," he says. "I love shiny white walls and the way the streetlights throw fantastic shadows on them." He also likes the quality of wood in the stripped window frames and old folding porch chairs, which, combined with a potted fan palm, soften and give color relief to the interior. His apartment is open, welcoming, an ideal place to do the entertaining he so much enjoys. The ample space has the cheerful polish of the designer's thoroughly contemporary, solid approach to technology and its many products.

Where Michael Schaible's apartment turns inward, oriented to the social pleasures of home, Robert Bray's Manhattan studio is completely oriented to the outside—the spectacular view and the natural light. The basic vocabulary is the same, however: carpeted platforms, a cantilevered table, white walls, a large plant, beach chairs. There are almost no objects, and the windows are bare. "I love beautiful things, but I don't develop attachments. For instance, I don't even have a bookshelf, and I read like a fiend. But when I read something, I always think of some friend I'd like to pass the book on to. I also give objects away. That's my way of keeping things going and acquiring new material at the same time."

Indeed, new materials represent one key to Bray-Schaible, even though they avoid a facile attraction to novelty in their work. Instead, the two designers have a keen awareness that many utilitarian objects and materials in fact exhibit the highest quality of design. Tread plate, laminated plastic and enamelized steel may not be the most dazzling inventions, but they have practical surfaces that contribute textural interest.

Bray-Schaible interiors—for all the drama of their unrelenting straight lines, flat surfaces and abrupt black-white contrasts—never suggest austerity. They are, with their mixture of elements and their straightforward appeal, always animated and exciting, and remarkably stylish.

"I love beautiful things, but I don't develop attachments."

Bray

The Bray Residence

In Robert Bray's studio—a multilevel and multipurpose environment—industrial materials imaginatively used contribute a functional aesthetic. Industrial carpeting minimizes the need for furniture. The framelike sculpture on the laboratory table is by Bruno Ameda. Beach chairs near the windows add transparency and lightness.

29

"I love shiny white walls and the way the streetlights throw fantastic shadows on them."

Schaible

The Schaible Residence

ABOVE: A suede-upholstered Le Corbusier armchair and a mattress wrapped in channel-quilted canvas make for a simplified seating/sleeping arrangement in the studio. Indicative of the décor's flexibility is a Randy Green photograph placed casually against a wall.

OPPOSITE: In Michael Schaible's versatile living/dining room, the back of a steel bookcase functions as a space divider and banquette backrest. Specifically designed adjustable lighting introduces linear accents, which are reinforced by vertical blinds.

*ABOVE: Entertaining is improvisational in the living/din-
ing room, where shiny porcelain-topped restaurant pedestal
tables can be placed in any part of the room for dinner
parties. Softly illuminating the tablesetting are a pair of
hurricane lamps, transformed from industrial battery jars.*

*OPPOSITE: Radius-cornered mirrors brighten the window-
less bedroom, adding light, sparkle and a reflection of the
living/dining room window. A carpeted platform elevates
the bed amid bouquets of lilies, real, reflected and shadowy.*

Eleanor S. Brown

Eleanor Brown

*"I try to design rooms around their
architecture or to create architecture
for rooms where none exists."*

"You drift from something minor—a way to pass your time, with one little assistant to help— and eventually it becomes really something," says Mrs. Archibald Brown, summing up her lengthy career as a New York interior designer and founder, in 1924, of McMillen. Her words need a gloss, however: Mrs. Brown moves and works with grace, but she doesn't actually "drift," physically or metaphorically. And "really something" should be interpreted as involving not only McMillen's own ability to keep abreast of change over sixty years but also its capacity to do so without abandoning its founder's standards—respect for tradition and excellence of workmanship.

To Mrs. Brown, interior design long ago became second nature. Her fellow designer and admirer the late Billy Baldwin once said, "She considers decoration not only as an end in itself but as part of a way of life." Anyone who knows her understands that she is by nature as disinclined to dictate about décor as about living. Yet her experience and reputation are such that she is often consulted as an oracle, and (if only in self-defense) she is prepared to mention a few of the principles that have guided her career. "Rooms should reflect the personality of their owner," she says. "Best for a decorator to resist the temptation of producing a pretentious or novel effect. Pretention palls; fads fade."

All of her homes and working headquarters have borne her gentle but perceptible imprint. Perhaps, however, it is her country house, *Four Fountains*, at Southampton, Long Island, that provides the most telling example of her architectural and decorative approach. The house was originally designed and built for a client in 1930 by Mrs. Brown's second husband, the late Archibald M. Brown, a well-known architect. The client was rather unusual in wanting a dilettante's pleasure dome near the ocean, not a conventional seaside house. In addition, he required a private hall where he could entertain his friends with amateur theatricals, films and concerts. In 1942, when World War II was on and amateur theatricals were off, the property came on the market. Mr. and Mrs. Brown decided to buy it and convert the pleasure dome into a summer house of their own.

It was a daring decision for the period. The extravaganza of the 1930s had turned into a 1940s white elephant. Its conversion entailed the transformation of a vast interior area into a habitable living room, and required the substitution of two double bedrooms with baths for what had once been a raised stage; moreover, a large church organ had to be removed from the area.

"It was an extraordinary achievement, miles ahead of its time in concept," was Billy Baldwin's judgment. "Functional intimacy" is how yet another old friend and frequent houseguest, the late artist and designer Van Day Truex, described the unique quality of Four Fountains, which he considered the best handling of all-purpose space that he knew.

Throughout the house, the furniture is predominantly eighteenth-century French and Italian. Fabric colors are mild by current standards but agreeably unemphatic and easy on the eye, never precious or weak. According to Mrs. Brown, the furniture "was just an accumulation of the things we had. We bought very little. In the years that I have lived here, I have only re-covered the sofas and chairs once—and in the same colors as before. But my friends, even the young ones, seem to think the place is more or less all right."

Her reference to the approval of the young is revealing. At McMillen, much of the contemporary designing is confidently entrusted to the younger members of the staff—with happy results. Understanding breeds understanding, and confidence inspires confidence. One doesn't have to be an evergreen nonagenarian to know that good plants grow from good roots.

"It was an extraordinary achievement," said Billy Baldwin, *"miles ahead of its time."*

ABOVE: The seven-acre Southampton estate features a circular courtyard fringed with boxwood and cryptomeria.

OPPOSITE: Prominent in the 40-foot-square living room is a round Louis XVI Italian table, a set of Louis XV French armchairs and an Italian Empire console.

ABOVE AND RIGHT: A long Italian Empire fruitwood table displays collectibles and functions as part of a freestanding partition.

ABOVE: *The large living room contains a cheerful dining area that overlooks a verdant landscape.*

OPPOSITE: *This and another bedroom were created by enclosing the stage area of the private theater that had been the main structure. The antique bed is Spanish.*

Diane Burn Eden

Diane Burn

"I walk into a space and try to see what the space calls for, what it calls for you to do."

Gleaming white and Italianate, the Henry Casebolt house on the hilltop was *the* manor of the neighborhood when it was completed in 1866. The neighborhood has changed considerably over the past century, and it is now the choicest of San Francisco residential locales. The pastures, barn and windmill are gone, along with—alas—the rustic lake with waterfall and island. Yet with its hilltop situation and substantial size, the house still dominates the immediate surroundings, a picturesque presence among its more conventionally handsome neighbors.

It is a house to weave Gothic tales about, and it seems appropriate that it was acquired by Diane Burn, a young romantic who never doubted, from the moment she first came upon the then-occupied house in the early 1970s, that it would someday be hers. And so it is still, more than a decade later, even though her interior design career has taken her to New York. Rented and well cared for, it remains just as she left it, an enchanting anachronism; for out of a nineteenth-century family home built to accommodate eleven children, Diane Burn created a fantasy world that calls to mind earlier felicities.

Here are an eighteenth-century French country kitchen with time-stained, crumbling stucco walls and handpainted beamed ceiling; a dining room that suggests a Renaissance courtyard; a living room that is more a ballroom, all eighteenth-century boiseries and mirrored panels. And then there is the master bedroom, the stuff of storybooks, with two hundred yards of gauze flowing from a baldachin over the bed.

For Miss Burn, from the first, the house was a highly charged experience. The romance began with her discovery of the house, which had been occupied for the past forty years by the same family; nevertheless, every so often she would drive by for another glimpse, until almost inevitably— it now seems in retrospect—a For Sale sign appeared. At last she was able to enter interiors she felt she could already imagine.

Once inside, however, she discovered that the reality beyond the door belied the exterior. "The interiors were the worst example of Victorian I'd ever seen in my life," she says. Although there were fourteen-foot ceilings, there were no moldings, nothing of interior architectural interest. Even the stairway, with its spindly balustrade, was considered meager.

She was determined to have it just the same. "I had dreamed of having this house. I just *knew* it was my house," she says. And she did indeed make it fully hers, putting her whole heart into it for several years; she was in no hurry at all to finish shaping the interiors.

For Miss Burn, the design process is always an emotional experience. Her favorite aspects are the structural and interior finishes, and her means are ethereal wall washes, *faux-marbre* painted fantasies, eighteenth-century boiseries, moldings, walls of mirror, tented and handpainted ceilings. The romantic effects are furthered by lighting. Candlelight is the basic light for evening entertaining, and all of the period chandeliers are on dimmers to simulate the look of candlelight.

Throughout the lengthy design process she gathered together a nucleus of artists and craftsmen who became as absorbed as she was in the creative activity of making a unique statement of this house. Sean McVey worked with Diane Burn in creating the wall finish and the painted wood-beamed ceiling for the kitchen. He also created the delicate wash for the dining room walls and the rusticated walls of the foyer, introduced to continue the mood of the exterior. Ami Magill created a panorama of painted-finish extravaganzas for the house, most spectacularly the ostensibly inlaid marble floor in the dining room.

Diane Burn wasn't burdened by the usual practical considerations of seating and furniture placement. Guests might have been invited to stroll through the formal Italianate dining room—a room designed as a direct transition from the Corinthian-columned exterior—and on into the eigh-

teenth-century country kitchen. There they would
spend the evening on wood benches flanking the
heavy table, a fire glowing in the hearth and candles flickering overhead.

Or the guests might have found themselves
in the living room, candlelight shining from mirrored walls and glowing boiseries. Miss Burn likes
this room best "when it is completely empty and
we have a big party for about three hundred
people"—a dance to the music of time, perhaps.

Everything about the house seems personally significant for Diane Burn. Across the driveway is a nineteenth-century wrought iron gate
that she found herself. It happened to fit perfectly
and was worked with the initial *D*. After all, wasn't
someone named Diane Burn going to be looking
for just such a flourish for her house?

*ABOVE: Completed in 1866 for the Henry Casebolt family,
the Italianate house stands amid a flourishing garden.*

*RIGHT: Fourteen-foot walls in the living room are detailed
with 18th-century boiserie washed in three pastel shades.
Arched mirrored panels and tall draped windows soften the
boiserie geometry, while original flooring provides a hard
bottom plane. Period French furniture is accented by the
terra-cotta countenance of Diane de Poitiers.*

44

"I had dreamed of having this house. I just knew it was my house."

ABOVE: The kitchen evokes a rustic and inviting 18th-century French country example, complete with a massive carved French mantel above a large open hearth, an 18th-century French oak vintner's table and a Parisian Belle Epoque baker's table heaped with provincial harvest baskets. The painting is by Ami Magill.

RIGHT: A Pompeian-style bronze pig appears to leap toward the veritable Lucullan feast arranged atop the stone and marble dining table. Walls are washed with subtle faux-marbre *veining,* while flooring is painted to approximate Florentine inlaid marble.

46

LEFT: Artist Ami Magill painted the master bedroom floor in the style of Louis XV.

BELOW LEFT: Delicate French dentelle hangings shelter an amusing Directoire copper tub in the master bath.

OPPOSITE: The master bedroom is a realm of alluring feminine enchantment. Two hundred yards of gauze lavishly drape the Louis XV lit à la polonaise, while unbleached muslin softly filters the light through tall windows.

Steve Chase

*"I have obviously been inspired by
many architects. There is Luis
Barragán in the colors and the great
walls; Gaudí in some of the chair
designs; and Frank Lloyd Wright in
the plan, but I have always tried to
reinterpret the ideas within my own
vocabulary of form."*

If the final test of architecture is its ability to transcend time by becoming a magnificent ruin, the new Steve Chase residence in Rancho Mirage, California, has the necessary prerequisites. Great earth-colored walls intersect one another and end in steps that descend into the desert. The house behind those walls, together with immense cacti, slabs of stone, and rocks, creates a place that seems governed by geologic time.

The house is the result of a close collaboration between interior designer Steve Chase and the architects Richard Holden and William Carl Johnson of Palm Desert. The project is a showcase of splendor and devotion to the art of habitation. Palaces, villas and temples of the past inevitably come to mind. "The temple was a place where people went for spiritual inspiration," says Steve Chase. "For me, architecture fulfills this purpose."

The architectural order of the house is established by means of large columns, while as an echo, the garden manifests a natural order through the use of pillarlike saguaro cactus. Masterfully, Steve Chase has expanded his usual arena of operation to include both the garden and the architecture in a new concept of the interior. The use of man-made and natural columns is not the only aspect of this expansion. The large slabs of aggregate for the floor and walkways inside and out, combined with an abundance of rocks, makes the ground plane a single articulated room.

The house sits at the foot of the Santa Rosa Mountains on the southern slope of the Coachella Valley. "I wanted to live next to the mountains and the desert I have hiked in over the last twenty years," says Steve Chase. "My new house had to be ordered, planned and closer to the austerity of the landscape. I wanted mainly two materials, the stuccoed wall and the stone floor. Great open space. A house without compromises."

The roofed part of the house is cruciform. Service areas and bedrooms extend along one axis, public rooms and entertainment areas reach out along the other. The furnishings are set against sumptuous leather walls, granite, and fine stucco. Throughout, there is an extensive collection of contemporary paintings and sculpture, yet a domestic feeling prevails. The living areas are like piazzas with places for rest, eating and entertainment. The décor is pure Steve Chase: elegant, colorful and very comfortable.

The cruciform plan of the house creates four gardens. Next to the entry garden, secluded behind a giant slab of a wall, lies a private refuge dotted with ocotillos set in a mock desert. The others are dominated by the saguaro and rocks. Beside the pool, placed between these two gardens, are four dramatic reclining chairs of cement, on tile bases.

If the visual power of the home derives from the various man-made and natural columns, the plan provides conceptual power. The floor dominates: the third dimension is really an extension of area, and the ceiling—a mere skin—is repeatedly violated to admit light. Finally, the ground plane appears as a fantasy map of an enchanted geography far beyond the humdrum of everyday life. Islands of rest and luxury in the shape of great overstuffed chair-beds, tables large and small, and unusual seating make it possible to turn this quiet personal oasis into a bustling palace of life. Says Steve Chase modestly, while smiling broadly, "I'm just the caretaker here."

"My new house had to be ordered, planned, and closer to the austerity of the landscape— a house without compromises."

ABOVE: At the entrance, squares of glass block articulate and establish scale with earth-toned walls. The sculpture is by Jerry Peart.

RIGHT: The living room reveals the open, fluid plan of the interior. Paintings are by Ronald Davis (left) and Laddie John Dill (right); the sculpture is by Michael Todd.

RIGHT: A view of the dining room seen from the living room culminates in a Japanese screen by Shiryu Morita. Resting on the buffet beneath it is a wooden bowl by Ed Moulthrop. The painting is Ronald Davis's Slab and Bar Nebula, *and the steel sculpture is Brian Skelton's* Column. *Dining room chairs, set about two tables, are upholstered in leather.*

BELOW RIGHT: The patio off the living room affords a view of the pool area, gazebo, guest house and, not least, the Santa Rosa Mountains. Faux stone patio furnishings unify interior and exterior.

LEFT: Stepped walls of glass block partially enclose the gazebo. The chairs, reminiscent of Gaudí, are of tile. The ceiling mural is by Andre Miripolsky.

BELOW LEFT: The master bedroom combines a sense of luxury with an earthy feeling. A rug of suede, resembling wood shavings, creates an island of texture for the leather-covered bed and chaise longue. A sculpture by Joyce Kohl complements a Robert Natkin painting.

FOLLOWING PAGES: Reclining chairs of cement and tile are solidly ensconced poolside. The architectonic sculpture is by Guy Dill. A patinated copper roof majestically crowns the jewellike gazebo.

Leo Dennis *Jerry Leen*

Leo Dennis   Jerry Leen

*"Museums influenced us greatly. In
European museums you see the very
best . . . Your eye becomes used
to that, and that's what you
begin to relate to."*

"I can walk into an antiques shop," says Jerry Leen, "glance around and in one instant spot something that has a special spirit, a distinction. It is as if you planted a row of tulips: most of them will be all right, but one or two will have a stature that is straight, with an air of elegance."

"When we shop," says his partner, Leo Dennis, "we walk about fifteen miles a day. It's my pleasure. It's interesting to buy everything that pleases you. We can do that because we have an outlet. A private person would get to a point where he couldn't manage it."

The two designers and antiquarians of impeccable taste have created a shop that attracts many customers—among them any number of designers. "It all started years ago," Mr. Leen says. "Leo and I met at the Santa Barbara Museum sale and began talking. I was working on Sunset Boulevard with Violet Searcy and Buddy Robart, top designers at the time, and Leo was in real estate. He came by and eventually got involved with the shop. I went into landscaping, and he started working with Violet. In a while we decided to open a shop."

They went to Europe, bought a car and with no itinerary, spent nine months driving around. "We spent time in museums, where we played a game," says Mr. Dennis; "we pretended we could have anything in the museum we wanted, and we put together imaginary rooms. You know, we could use anything that existed in the world—and possibly we used things that didn't."

They returned to open a shop in Los Angeles, where they did everything themselves, covering the walls with rough-hewn redwood, which no one had done in those days. They created an unpretentious background, then brought in glorious things and let them speak for themselves.

Today Dennis & Leen is located in an old winery on Robertson Boulevard in Los Angeles. Chandeliers from many ages and countries hang from unfinished rafters. On a plaster wall is an oval garden urn taken from Versailles during the French Revolution. Eighteenth-century fabrics just arrived from Indonesia, Persia and Afghanistan are piled on a handsome Chinese lacquered table.

They have culled items from the best in Europe for the shop; culled again from the shop are treasures for their own residences. Not surprisingly, in the Los Angeles apartment where Jerry Leen lived until a few years ago, there was not a superfluous line. The space was treated with the discipline of Vivaldi: the design was hard, precise, with many fascinations. While the structure was neither high ceilinged nor architecturally grand, the interiors were so skillfully designed that visitors were unaware of anything but a compelling quiet amid interesting qualities. At a glance there was refinement and complexity.

Royal African grass cloth was used next to Venetian taffeta; Genoese cut velvet covered an Austrian Baroque chair, its back upholstered in burlap. An elaborate console was arranged with lead and early Ming bronze, early silver and crystal. A cool elegance was apparent everywhere. About such juxtapositions, Mr. Leen says, "It's like going into a garden and seeing something fragile, like a narcissus, and next to it a cactus or a succulent that has bravado and virility and strength. Each thing has its own magic."

For Mr. Leen there is magic in many things, including a certain time of day. "The most marvelous time for me," he says, "is after the business hours, in the evening when I come home and sit overlooking the garden. I have a light cocktail and thoughts come to me and my mind seems free. There is a tranquillity that clarifies and washes away all those surface things. Then other thoughts come forth. It is a time of joy in which I delight."

Says Mr. Dennis of his Los Angeles apartment, in which he displays his collections with great enjoyment, "In the right circumstances, I'd be ten times more elaborate. I'd like a room all in oak paneling, with rock crystal chandeliers hanging from fifteen-foot ceilings. I have things from every part of the world. I don't care if

"In the right circumstances, I'd be ten times more elaborate."

Dennis

something is old or not, or where it came from. I like things first for their form, second for their color and third for their quality.

"I think people make a big mistake looking for quality only," he continues. "You can find it, for example, in a big Dutch marquetry cabinet, but it might be hideously ugly. The form is wrong; very often the color is bad. People get all this quality together and don't understand why their houses look terrible. They say, 'I've done the right thing; I bought quality.'"

Ultimately, taste is the only dependable answer, according to Mr. Dennis. Dennis & Leen is the creation of two discriminating designers who freely appreciate with wit and sensitivity the arts of the entire world.

The Dennis Residence

OPPOSITE ABOVE: A William Kent console bears an 11th-century Persian bowl and a Han vase; behind it is a framed Venetian fresco.

OPPOSITE BELOW: The iron legs of the 18th-century dining room table terminate in cannonballs; the chairs are in the style of Louis XIV. A chunk of ornamental stone on the glass tabletop tints the subtle setting.

ABOVE: Two 18th-century Pierre Puget wood figures survey an international mix of objects in Leo Dennis's living room. A maharaja's snakeskin walking stick, encrusted with gold and diamonds, rests on an Egyptian stool. Chairs are Régence and Italian Directoire. On the Belgian Louis XVI oak table rests a carved-wood pith helmet—an Ashanti crown.

The Leen Residence

OPPOSITE: *Large Chinese and Korean portraits and a 17th-century carved wood shogun, on the adjacent terrace, lend their serene countenances to the bedroom's rich furnishings. The chairs and commode are Régence.*

In the living room 17th-century Spanish Colonial gilded stone finials flank an 18th-century Neapolitan sofa; above it is a Piranesi watercolor. Two Charles II side chairs and an Italian Directoire armchair complete the seating group.

"It is like going into a garden and seeing something fragile, like a narcissus, and next to it a cactus or a succulent that has bravado, virility and strength."

Leen

ABOVE: *In Jerry Leen's living room, T'ang camels accent a Ming desk. Below stands an ancient vase from Crete. The painting is by Duri Amatzu.*

OPPOSITE: *A large 17th-century Italian marble bust and a Pompeian-style bronze deer take part in the composition of the compact dining room, seen largely in reflection.*

Michael de Santis

Michael de Santis

"When I see something I like, I buy it. I'm not the kind of person who spends five hours selecting an ashtray."

New York in the 1980s: glamorous and tawdry, gorgeous and harsh, a city that has everything. A city whose complex, unruly life teems through streets laid out in the orderly pattern of a grid. A city so colorful and so full of contrasts that its spirit, as expressed in a room, can perhaps be encompassed only by the abstractions of black and white. No doubt with this in mind—and with a keen awareness of the particular time and place in which he works—interior designer Michael de Santis has created an apartment for himself atop one of New York's tall buildings.

Manhattan, of course, is most glamorous by night, and so it is only fitting that the designer's apartment be seen to best advantage once the sun has dipped below the horizon. "It's basically a night apartment," Michael de Santis admits. "I work during the day and weekend at my house in Easthampton. I don't entertain much here; I do most of my entertaining in the country. When I'm alone here, I might just order Chinese food and sit in the living room, eat, listen to music and look out at all the lights. But when I do have people in—especially people from out of town— it's very nice for them, because *this is New York.*" That it most assuredly is, from the expansive view to the interior décor itself. "I did the living room in black so that the walls wouldn't be over- powered by the view, and vice versa," the designer explains. The color/no color scheme takes center stage even as it stands back to let visitors admire the panorama of buildings, bridges, and sky.

The living room itself almost seems like a distillation of the city night, full of the spirit of adventure and romance. These feelings are emphasized by the large square of black mirror topping a table; the room, in reflection, plunges into its nocturnal depths. A wall painted matte black and speckled with white translates into a starry sky, while against it, a Sorenson painting reads almost as black lightning limned in silver.

Glinting here and there are luxurious acces- sories Michael de Santis has chosen with a sure instinct. Indeed, his choices, here sparingly deployed, bespeak the visual equivalent of perfect pitch. There are prisms, Lucite objects of a faintly Egyptian cast, etched-glass pyramids, and a sen- suously contoured blown-glass vase acquired in Venice. About these, too, there is something essentially "New York," at once simple and sophis- ticated. All share a crystalline clarity—not of water but rather of some rare, costly liqueur whose ascetic appearance barely hints at its exotic flavor.

If all of the accessories are predominantly geometric, the sumptuously proportioned sofa and chairs are all smooth curves and soft, deep cush- ions. Upholstered in light-hued flannel almost the color of moonlight, they appear almost buoyant against the dark background. Amid these dramatic abstractions of black and white, the rainbow spectrum of city life is clearly caught in a neon sculpture's intertwining tubes, the one touch of color in the room.

The bedroom, reached by a mirror-lined corridor, is more intimate in tone than the living room, and less intense. Silver and bone subside into warm gray lacquer, while curved corners are favored over sharp right angles. Visually striking, the bedroom is practical as well. "Everything," the designer points out, "works from the bedside control panels." For the effects of lighting he uses surface fixtures.

Considering his apartment as a whole, Michael de Santis says, "It's neither masculine nor feminine. It simply has a contemporary look. To me, New York is becoming more contemporary every day. I find it a marvelous place to live. Cer- tainly I wouldn't have done a place like this in Los Angeles, for example." No, indeed. Only for New York will these colors and this tone do. Using them, he has achieved a design that skillfully mir- rors the time and place in which he lives.

"I did the living room in black so that the walls wouldn't be overpowered by the view, and vice versa."

PRECEDING PAGES AND ABOVE: An achromatic palette and sleek surfaces give the living room a quintessentially nighttime-in-Manhattan flavor. Surrounded by a flannel-upholstered sofa and chair, a stark glass and steel table presents a mélange of forms. Reflected in the mirrored wall, a hand-thrown pottery vase filled with alliums contributes fanciful color atop a lacquered pedestal. Behind the sofa, Don Sorenson's Black Painting creates a blizzard of light.

OPPOSITE: A neon sculpture by Paul Seide emblazons the dining area with color. Flannel-covered chairs surround the parchment and stainless-steel table. The understated flatware has an unusual provenance: the designer purchased it aboard the Concorde while flying from New York to Paris.

In the master bedroom, smooth
contours and sumptuous fabrics convey sensuous warmth.
Deep-hued velvet covers the
walls and bed, while a chair is
upholstered in stenciled suede.
Near it, Arturo Di Modica's
sculpture of polished bronze,
titled Ecstasy, gleams evoca-
tively. The acrylic painting
by Jay Whitehead ignites the
room's palette. A soffit of lacquered steel conceals lighting
fixtures, while vertical blinds,
partially open, reveal Manhattan's glittering panorama.

Rubén de Saavedra

Rubén de Saavedra

*"If I'd lived in the eighteenth century,
I'd have been an architect."*

A warm, pervasive flow of light and strong color plays across polished, glazed and mirrored surfaces. Myriad reflections and refined furnishings and objects contrast with roughly woven Arab rugs. The whole is again reflected in brilliantly lacquered ceilings. The audacious use of reds, blues and ochres is reminiscent of a Spanish palace and reveals a baroque eclecticism and unwavering eye for true quality of surface, line, color and proportion. These elements are all there working in Rubén de Saavedra's New York apartment.

The designer's deft hand at assembling such strikingly assertive pieces comes from a profound understanding of the grandeur of seventeenth- and eighteenth-century European taste. This is a sophisticated look, and one that can't be rushed. To be a designer, in Mr. de Saavedra's mind, is the same as being an artist. The only difference is the format of the work. For him, the interior design field has fertile possibilities as a vital part of daily life. "Designs get better as people become more educated, travel, see and demand more of the creators of their environments," he says; "and I consider myself a creator."

Rubén de Saavedra had no sooner graduated from the New York School of Design with honors than he found himself with one of America's foremost actors, Paul Muni, playing the role of his first client. It was a little overwhelming at first, but he realized that the experience opened many doors and freed something in his spirit right at the beginning. Since Paul Muni was color-blind, that particular assignment was proof by fire for a man so in tune with color.

Mr. de Saavedra's use of color is decidedly not simple. His theme of boldly colored settings comes not from tinted walls and draperies but from startlingly bright objects that reflect and animate complex surfaces. In his own home, each piece of his wide and ever-growing collection of ceramics, bronzes, terra-cottas, lacquers, rugs and *objets de vertu* contributes its color and personality to the setting. He is an indefatigable collector.

"But," he says, "I wouldn't go so far as to take the Elgin Marbles home with me, even if the British Museum would let me. That would be collecting on far too grand and imposing a scale." He did, however, take home a rare seventeenth-century Venetian stone bust of a Moor, vividly painted and sporting a gold earring; a marvelously equivocal piece he describes as "a Brancusi airplane propeller"; and a fine pedestal by Clodion. Surveying his collections, he says, "I know it must appear as if my mind's a clutter, but remember—collecting deals with my heart."

He has the curiosity of a collector. An unexpectedly beautiful house seen while traveling irresistibly draws him to see the inside, to see whether there will be an added surprise. So he will often ring the bell and gain admission.

"All experiences are important," he says. "Today, tomorrow and yesterday help you understand different ways of living. Then you evaluate what is best for yourself and do it." Rubén de Saavedra never settles for what he already knows.

He constantly draws, and finds his drawings an immediate and intimate exposure of a mind filled with the schemes and fantasies of a true dreamer. His aim is totality reached through unified effort, through knowing where you're starting from and through keeping your eye on where you're going—not by pushing furniture about and letting things happen. "That's amateur hour," he says. "The eleventh commandment should be, 'Thou shalt have a decorator.'"

He never feels his apartment or his way of life should be forced on his clients, however. It couldn't be. He can be as comfortable in creating an updated French or English interior as in creating some marvelous Chinese illusion. There are no restricting prejudices.

A client once asked for an apartment done only in white, red and blue. Instead of feeling hindered by these limitations of choice, he saw the challenging possibilities of what was a puzzle to solve, and he transformed a restriction into an

> **"Designs get better as people become more educated, travel, see and demand more of the creators of their environments."**

inspiration. "After all," he remarks, "the American flag is not *just* red, white and blue."

Though his aims are always clear and he knows when they have been achieved, he does not want his clients to feel that when a job is finished, that's the end. He wants them to know they can rely on him; if clients find they want to elaborate or continue a theme as they evolve, he is there to help. The designer has the added pleasure of seeing others develop through his influence, "not because of me," he says, "but because of themselves. Once they are introduced to new vistas, it often happens. They simply take off."

Mirrored folding doors open to reveal part of a sophisticated mise-en-scène in the living room. Raised high on an ancient Aswan stone column—and seen in reflection—is a 17th-century Venetian bust. A bronze Bacchus on a marble mount, by Clodion, rests on the Louis XV bureau plat.

ABOVE: Deep-toned walls and richly textured surfaces set off 18th-century French furnishings in the living room. Highlights include the gilded Régence mirror and the Directoire table. The painting of a woman is by Jean-Pierre Cassigneul. The table laden with porcelain objects reflects the designer's penchant for collecting.

OPPOSITE: The Louis XVI table in the dining room is set with regal 1805 Sèvres plates, while other porcelain items are displayed in the secrétaire à l'Anglais, also Louis XVI. A terra-cotta pedestal by Clodion supports a bust by Pajou. The landscape is by Bernard Klene.

78

Tailored warmth, enhanced by bold color, permeates the master bedroom. A period mirrored commode à la perruque *shares the mix with a Tunisian rug and South Seas batik wallpaper.*

Angelo Donghia

Angelo Donghia

*"All I could think of when I was
preparing the house was the way
I like to live—with light and air
and a sense of being part
of the environment."*

Houses can be like certain human beings. Once they enter the consciousness, nothing can erase them. When New York interior designer Angelo Donghia went to Key West, Florida, for the first time about a decade ago, he decided to spend an afternoon looking at various properties on the island. "It's a particular hobby of mine," he explains. "There's no better way to understand the meaning of a place."

When he saw one late-Victorian house with delicate wooden columns and an eccentric conical roof, his decision was immediate: "I bought it." After returning to New York, however, he canceled what seemed to him to have been a rather impetuous choice. "And I didn't think too much about it," he says. "Then, a few months later, a friend called me and said quite casually, 'Oh, Angelo, remember the house you almost bought? It's finally been sold.' 'But it's mine!' I wailed, realizing that I'd wanted it all along. Well, many complicated negotiations later, I had a termite-riddled, disintegrating wreck of a house on my hands—lovely though it still was."

The excitement of looking beyond the ruined face of a house to detect the essential aristocracy of its features is what makes restoration worthwhile, and Mr. Donghia does indeed have that discernment. Today the house, which is now owned by fashion designer Calvin Klein, floats in creamy detachment, framed in tropical foliage—a fastidious restoration that mirrors the past but is filled with the luminous air of the present.

"Obviously one is operating on many levels in a project like this," Mr. Donghia says. "There is an element of the human personality that is attracted to land, to buildings, as representatives of power and permanence. There is also the delight in salvaging something beautiful that would otherwise be destroyed." Mr. Donghia's point of view has always seemed both urban and urbane. His city spaces have invariably been luxurious and more than a little worldly. The challenge has often been to achieve a great deal from unpromising beginnings. In the Key West house, however, the designer took another approach from precisely the opposite direction.

"I restored the house by stripping it and reducing everything to its most natural, primitive state," he explains. "Really, design can be seen ultimately as dealing with a six-sided box: four walls, a ceiling and a floor. The latter two are usually neglected or disregarded. Treating all these surfaces equally is intrinsic to the way I work. And in this case, I treated them in the most honest—which is to say, the most absolutely simple—way, to stay close to the original concept of the house. Everything came down to taking out as much as possible and leaving the shell." The image of the shell comes up frequently in Mr. Donghia's descriptions of the house. It was empty, resonant, glowing, like the inside of a conch.

"Having stripped everything down to its most basic form," he says, "I would have been content to live in the rooms as they were—quite bare. Their proportions were so fine, the windows placed so sensitively, that I could have moved in happily and just existed in a very minimal, spiritual way." Yet the furniture that he placed in the wide, cool rooms seemed anything but obtrusive. Bamboo and wicker predominated, and floated naturally in the generous, uncluttered spaces.

"The architect placed the house, which incidentally is on the highest point of the island—fourteen feet!—so lovingly and at such a perfect angle to catch the trade winds that I didn't need air conditioning. Instead, there were many fans turning lazily during the afternoons. When I'm in a tropical environment, I want to feel it."

As with many things simple and effective, the pleasures of the house revealed themselves almost shyly. Indicative of Mr. Donghia's understated design was the fact that the floors, stained white on the ground floor, were echoed by walls in which the raw wood had been subtly modified by a rubbing of white paint into the grain. "Of course I took some license here and there," the designer smiles. "I couldn't resist adding moldings and painting them high-gloss white."

*"I restored the house by stripping
and reducing everything to its
most natural, primitive state."*

"This house was unlike anything I had ever done. It was not just a pretty house; it was not only a place to indulge in feeling attractive and comfortable. It was also part of a new way of looking at myself—of paring down. I think we had all decorated ourselves to death in the preceding ten years, and it was time to assert the fact that purity of form, lightness and simplicity were important aims. And you know, imperfection is exhilarating." The designer also believes that certain intangibles are as important as the physical arrangement of rooms: "The way a curtain moves in the breeze, the way a rug is arranged, the distinctive scent of a special person. These are all terribly elusive things, yet I wanted them all to resonate at Key West."

The fact that he chose to leave so much appealingly blank was part of the beauty of the house. "There's a great deal I could say about the island of Key West," says Angelo Donghia, "that would help explain the spirit in which I created these rooms. All the qualities, the psychological effects of an island are here. There's a richness, an ambiguity—even a sort of decadence—that's unlike anything else in the United States."

All these influences were evident in the thoughtful and intelligent way in which Angelo Donghia returned his former summer home to life in the twentieth century. Restraint and modesty were the predominant qualities manifested in Mr. Donghia's restoration. Everything fit with absolute tact and sureness into its enfolding background and evoked ease and harmony.

ABOVE: The sun porch, at the back of the house, and the garden beyond capture the flavor of the idyllic tropical island setting at Key West. Bamboo furniture, an umbrella and potted plants are complemented by a thicket of palms. Behind the garden is the pool area.

OPPOSITE: Restored and stripped down to its bare form, the late-Victorian summer home retains its charm.

In the living room, raw wood walls were rubbed with white
paint. The designer defined the seating by placing a rug on
the diagonal, creating a corner for conversation.

A guest room, painted a delicate pastel hue, is minimally adorned with casual furnishings and an assortment of intriguing objects. Vivid stripes add playfulness.

OPPOSITE: In the airy master bedroom, a lacquered ceiling fan whirs on hot days—in lieu of air conditioning. Lightly scaled Chinese tables and chairs lend Oriental overtones to the low horizontal look.

ABOVE: The pool pavilion is an enticing area for solitary sun worship or casual entertaining. Checkerboard-patterned tiles edge the clear pool with crisp contrasting detail.

Ted Graber

"I love people to say, 'I'll have to come back. I haven't seen everything yet.'"

"I don't have a favorite period," says California interior designer Ted Graber, whose West Los Angeles home holds objects from many countries around the world. The objects, however, do have one thing in common: they reflect a craftsman's appreciation for the nature of materials.

Mr. Graber, whose father was both antiquarian and cabinetmaker, came by this appreciation early. "When I was quite young, I apprenticed under cabinetmakers, finishers, upholsterers. I worked until I realized that this end of the business was not for me, and I told my father I wanted to be in the design field." So after art school, Ted Graber joined the firm of the late William Haines, the well-known interior designer. "In those days there were craftsmen in Los Angeles who could do anything. Because I had a thorough grounding in *how* to do something as well as in *what* to do, anything I dreamed up could be accomplished. I had the most intricate leatherwork done—tooling, lacing and covering."

Today Ted Graber's pleasure is still in the re-creation of those crafts that flourished centuries ago, and he calls upon an accomplished cabinetmaker who can carve as well as finish, paint and do lacquer work. For instance, he recently had a leaf made for an eighteenth-century penwork table. "It is intricate and tedious work, requiring great patience and skill." Mr. Graber's craft is needlepoint, and it is found on pillows and cushions throughout his house. Yarns are piled in a Dutch clothes press, and there is an eighteenth-century framed sampler on one of the walls. "One day I used a magnifying glass and was surprised to see that the patterns are in cross-stitch. I began playing around with the designs, and now I've done them all."

This penchant for expression has prompted his collection of chairs. "In most cases, chairs represent the fantasy of a particular period more than any other piece of furniture," the designer explains. "Here is a Chippendale; this one is Adam; this Regency; this Moroccan—and this my father designed," he says, pointing out one chair after another. "You know, I still run into people who say, 'I have one of Edgar Graber's chairs.' I find all the chairs here interesting, including the ones I make myself." One, a hostess chair, is a small, low piece with a back on which to rest an elbow. "You can turn all the way around in it and face every part of the room."

As might be expected, the house is intensely personal, with objects that Mr. Graber says amuse or give him pleasure. Nothing has been acquired by accident or without reason, and nothing has been carelessly arranged. The décor is as well thought out as a painter's canvas. There is a collection of malachite on one shelf, some crystal quartz with slivers of silver on an inlaid table. A collage of lace, ribbon and satin is in a hallway. "It reminds me a little of the state of Versailles before Gérald Van der Kemp took over the renovation—the eighteenth century blown apart!" There are also figures from the west coast of Africa: snake charmers, hunting dogs, alligators, men carrying bundles on their heads. "I picked those up in 1969, when I did the ambassador's residence in Regency Park. On weekends I'd go to the markets on Portobello Road." There is a Regency tea caddy and seashells; Japanese prints and a Chinese interpretation of an English falconer; the simplest Japanese plates; Queen Anne lacquered cabinets; English and French pewter. There is every color blending into an overall tonality. As with a puzzle, a thousand pieces make up the whole.

For Mr. Graber, the arrangement of objects can be as creative as the shaping of raw material. "When I finish a design project, I tell my clients, 'Above and beyond what I have done, the room will die if you do not keep it alive by adding to it yourself. You live here and you are the only ones who can really breathe life into it.' " The designer counts personal expression among mankind's many graces, and the rooms he creates bring out the best of his clients' capabilities—and his own.

*"In most cases, chairs represent
the fantasy of a particular period
more than any other piece of
furniture."*

*ABOVE: Humor pervades a corner where an 18th-century
portrait of a child joins a trio of singerie elements.*

*ABOVE RIGHT: English tea caddies flank the ferocious
beauty of a Medusa, focal point of a 19th-century Russian
door knocker. The painting, by Johannes Leemans, exhibits
exquisite trompe l'oeil artistry.*

*OPPOSITE: Beneath the painted gaze of a Turkish ambas-
sador, chairs in many styles reflect the designer's penchant
for this form. The hostess chair, fauteuils upholstered in
silk, and wheel-back chairs all have personalities.*

PRECEDING PAGES: Primitive sculptures lend intensity to the exotic mix of elements in the living room, where an animal theme is also evident.

LEFT AND BELOW LEFT: The dining room pays homage to the Classical Age: Its Regency table features Grecian figures in intricate penwork. Chairs by the designer's father, Edgar Graber, borrow from antiquity. A Roman bronze head, an 18th-century Apulian-style krater and a pair of toga-clad Meissen figurines gracefully accent the heroic theme. Artworks—a still life by René Genis and a painting by Wopon—add further appeal.

OPPOSITE: In the bedroom, a Queen Anne secretary with chinoiserie motifs complements the detailing of a mid-18th-century English armchair. The small canvas is by Celadada.

Bruce Gregga

Bruce Gregga

"My concept was to edit. Now every inch of the house is sharp line, all verticals and horizontals."

When Bruce Gregga says he is cleaning house, he does not mean scrubbing and sweeping. What the Chicago-based designer cleans best are the cluttered lines of a residence—by removing baseboards, trim and molding; solving the problem of exposed air conditioning units on a roof; simplifying a garden, straightening out an angled ceiling. These talents for organization came into play with the small house in Los Angeles that Mr. Gregga owned from 1977 to 1982, which he bought from the late film director George Cukor. Encompassing only 2,200 square feet, the six-room wood and stucco structure was one of three houses built on a portion of George Cukor's grand Hollywood estate that once served as a formal rose garden. (Katharine Hepburn occupied one of the houses for almost twenty years.)

Designed by Los Angeles architect John Woolf in the 1950s, the angular, flat-roofed house was a departure from Woolf's penchant for French Regency. "I don't know what the style was, exactly," says Bruce Gregga. "It wasn't Regency; it wasn't modern; it wasn't classical. Just clean lined." Though the designer did not purchase the property in order to redo it, his inclinations got the best of him. "It was really quite charming as it was—one of those places you could live in without even touching. It was very 1950s inside, with nice appointments and interesting lighting. But I couldn't resist the potential it offered."

The architect he engaged to make the desired changes never made an appearance, so "with the help of a fabulous Norwegian carpenter," he did all the architectural and design work himself. "We went right down to the studs." Mr. Gregga relocated the skylighted entrance hall in a central position where a windowed library once faced the driveway entrance. In addition, he altered the proportions of the octagonal living area by evening out the angled ceiling to twelve feet. Clean plaster lines intersected where the trim, baseboards and molding were removed. Sliding glass doors were replaced by tall French doors.

The Andes granite floors placed on the diagonal throughout the house were the result of a natural disaster. "The day we took the roof off to redo the living room ceiling, torrential rains began. Originally there were beautiful parquet floors but they soon became miserable washboards."

The diagonal pattern of the granite squares was repeated in the marble surrounding the pool and bordering the redwood teahouse in the garden, reaffirming the designer's efforts to maintain clean lines inside and out. The teahouse was his favorite project. He borrowed a book on Oriental architecture from the University of California, Los Angeles, pored over it and came up with the design. "All of the carving was done in the garage. Bottles of brandy and night meetings went into the making of that teahouse."

Removing the roof of the house for repairs had some happy consequences. "I looked up and saw the hills and the pine trees. I wanted to keep that, so we installed four skylights. When the moon was full and the stars were out on a clear Los Angeles night, it was quite magical."

By combining art objects from different periods in a contemporary and functional environment, Mr. Gregga reiterated his clean, uncomplicated plan for the house. Among his favorite pieces were rock crystals mounted on granite boxes in the entrance hall; the Giacometti andirons made from a maquette he admired in the sculptor's studio; a Louis XVI commode that once belonged to Colette, and a pair of mirrors from Somerset Maugham's *Villa Mauresque* in the south of France.

Bruce Gregga's passion for the clean line was apparent even in the kitchen, a streamlined study in black and white. "I love clean, clinical kitchens," he says. "For every client, I do a white kitchen. French or English porcelains, wood—everything looks good in such a context." Clearly there was little in this house that escaped the scrutiny of the designer's eye for organization.

"It's not Regency; it's not modern; it's not classical. Just clean lined."

PRECEDING PAGES: A central seating arrangement in the living room functions as an axis. Surrounding it are a gilt-wood console and mirror, a 19th-century Indian temple figure and a coromandel screen.

ABOVE: In the entrance hall, Lalanne sheep lend a pastoral note, which is reinforced by a view of a garden. A circular skylight captures the nuances of daylight.

RIGHT: Andes granite flooring in the dining room makes a dark foil for a Regency table surrounded by silk-upholstered chairs. A Züber panel contributes figurative delicacy.

ABOVE: Oriental architecture inspired the design of a garden teahouse that provides a shaded refuge from the sun.

ABOVE RIGHT: Exoticism flavors the versatile sitting room/bedroom. A virtuoso Cocteau drawing, a gift from film director George Cukor, accents a corner dominated by a Dutch marquetry desk ornamented with ivory.

BELOW RIGHT: The clarity of the décor extends to the bath, an exercise in simplicity. Amid grace notes of porcelain and silver, a window opens to a lacework of vines.

OPPOSITE: Above the Directoire daybed a circular window frames a leafy landscape. Small matching tables and a dauntless elephant on a faux-bois pedestal inject whimsy.

104

Albert Hadley (signature)

Albert Hadley

"A person becomes a designer because he has an intuitive flair, but he becomes a designer of merit through a long process of evolvement and involvement. The eye is what needs training, through care and constant investigation."

After a long series of projects, Albert Hadley is used to finding innovative solutions to difficult design problems in Manhattan. "My apartment there is in an unremarkable building," he says, "in a pleasant, though not architecturally outstanding, neighborhood, and the view is nothing to speak of. I was starting with a very familiar set of problems for the city dweller." Mr. Hadley is a modest man, much given to understatement and with a way of phrasing his sentences so that a great deal is said in few words. He is spare and articulate, and these traits are evident in the apartment he designed for himself in the late 1960s.

"I can tell you that this apartment represents many years of accumulation," he continues; "objects I've inherited, been given or have bought. But that was only a beginning. Now you can see what is left after a good deal of stringent editing. Here are the things that I feel comfortable with. One of the fascinating aspects of working in your own space is that over the years—once the initial pattern is set—individual pieces can be moved many times. And I like to think of life in the same terms: as an evolution, never as a static thing."

Yet Mr. Hadley is concerned with the overriding importance of that initial pattern. "The architecture of space seems to me critical. Furniture must be placed in such a way that these dynamics are respected. Successful design depends on being honest with the basics of a room. That isn't to say I don't try to improve a bad situation, but it doesn't seem to make any sense to try to transform a traditionally shaped room into a modern one. Still, there is more to good design than just making a room agreeable by filling it with fabrics and furniture. That would only be cosmetic. I'm fond of saying that 'design is total, decoration is embellishment.' To achieve the former, an intellectual eye is necessary."

The designer reached his present sense of assurance through several aesthetic incarnations. "I can remember my first apartment," he smiles. "It was all whitewashed, with brown felt sofas and horsehair chairs—and a black floor, of course. That was my no-color era. Then there was my Cecil Beaton period: all fine jewel colors. But gradually I evolved until I had enough self-knowledge to admit that I really preferred the happiest and most unforced of tonal values. In short, I am very much in favor of natural colors."

This calm understanding of a simple set of circumstances and a given repertory of needs is charted in the configurations of Mr. Hadley's living room. "It's a room with a wide variety of pleasures," he says, "from just gazing alone at the fire to being comfortable with guests." This inherent simplicity of vision has everything to do with his particular point of view, and like his personality, the space reveals itself slowly, growing in subtlety as further dimensions are brought into focus.

Recessed mirrored bases and cornices give the dark walls a floating quality. The designer neatly solved the problem of how to conceal heating and cooling elements by furring out the wall between the windows, thereby reducing everything to a single, unobtrusive grille. At the same time, this solution serves to make the windows deep recesses. The city is kept at an appropriate distance, and the room is given a sense of depth and solidity. A ceiling of Chinese tea paper forms an agreeable substitute for that diagram of beams so typical of the Manhattan apartment. In the same unobtrusive fashion, white doors slide into walls with a discreet technological murmur.

Mr. Hadley achieves remarkable feats of condensation through thoughtful structural design solutions. Into the single space of the hall, for example, there are no fewer than five different openings, but three of them are so artfully underplayed that they go unnoticed at first glance—unnoticed, but they are not disguised. While there is an element of trompe l'oeil in everything Mr. Hadley does, he would never dream of cheating. So all the doors are opened by visible wire pulls.

Another aspect of Mr. Hadley's philosophy that is given full rein in his apartment is the insis-

tence upon simplicity and modesty. "Those wire pulls are available in every good hardware store," he explains. "I didn't want anything custom-made.

"It does really come down to being truthful, doesn't it?" muses Mr. Hadley. "And it is so difficult to be completely honest with ourselves: I think we all want to do something that is radical and different, but that temptation should be overcome. What must be expressed is the strong thread of continuity in the pattern of life—that and our own particular preferences."

ABOVE: The well-honed totality incorporates an accumulation of cherished treasures. Satin-covered mid-18th-century Italian armchairs complement a contemporary sofa. The 17th-century floral still life is Dutch. To one side of the sofa is a table with a base in the form of a crouching human figure; it is early 18th century, of bleached pine.

OPPOSITE: An enigmatic giraffe regards its domain, where walls seem to float between mirrored recessed cornices and bases. The Chinese tea-papered ceiling and 17th-century mirror reflect subtle lighting.

"I think we all want to do something that is radical and different, but that temptation should be overcome."

ABOVE: *The study projects an intensely personal feeling with an amusing display of nostalgia and a functional space for work in the present. A gunmetal finial tops the lacquered bookcase, which was made in Berlin in 1928; the bookcase's gold, silver and copper decorations depict athletic events.*

OPPOSITE: *Late-18th-century American chairs flank a leather-topped Directoire mahogany writing table. Natural sisal matting covers bleached oak flooring.*

ABOVE AND ABOVE RIGHT: The master bedroom illustrates an adroit use of period pieces. Above the 17th-century English lacquered chest and the Regency demilune example are drawings by Hélène Fesenmaier. The French terra-cotta bust is from the 18th century.

An American Federal bull's-eye mirror reflects the late-18th-century English lacquered bed in the master bedroom.

Anthony Hail

"I finally decided if I like color so much in other homes, why don't I try it in my own?"

One short block on San Francisco's Russian Hill contrasts with the staggering slopes and sweeping vistas that mark this city by the bay. The street is level. Its houses, many of which were built in the nineteenth century, are fronted by trees and courtyard gardens. Interior designer Anthony Hail had long been attracted by the classic lines of one of these homes, and when it became available, he purchased it. "The façade reminds me of townhouses in northern Europe where I grew up," says the designer. "In renovating the structure, I wanted to maintain the feeling of a north European pavilion, with sun pouring in and cheerful colors."

The residence was built between 1860 and 1870, in the Victorian style. In 1911 Julia Morgan, architect of Hearst Castle, remodeled it, adding a new front wing that includes the present living room and the façade that first attracted Mr. Hail. Nothing remains of the Victorian exterior.

Anthony Hail renovated the home over a period of two and a half years, creating large rooms from many small ones and expanding doorways and windows to infuse dreary areas with light. He relocated doorways on the second story to provide a clear vista from one end of the floor to the other. The designer divided the house, which he owns with his business partner, Charles Posey, into two private living areas on separate floors. The partners use some rooms in common, including the living room and library. "The arrangement brings to mind European households in which generations of a family share the space and maintain private rooms as well," says Mr. Hail.

"There were structural obstacles I had to work around, including several immovable walls and chimneys, but I didn't mind that. It's more fun to work around obstacles than to sit down to an open board. The architectural firm of Walker & Moody did much of the layout and detail work. We saved every old door and scrap and put them back up, though often in new locations."

The designer, who studied architecture in college, is particularly fascinated with historical buildings. Thus, he was tempted to apply period ornamentation to his San Francisco home—elaborate cornices, bookcases and paneling. "But ultimately I decided to keep it understated and let the house speak for itself," he says. "I didn't want to 'Frenchify' the interior or bring to mind any particular period. For example, the double doors opening off each room are covered with eighteen coats of lacquer, like a piano. The panels on each door are differentiated by high-gloss, semigloss and matte finishes. It's a Scandinavian method and was done by craftsmen from Holland."

In his previous residences, Mr. Hail emphasized beige for interior backgrounds. Here he adopted a broader palette. From his former apartment he did, however, bring his extensive collections of antique furniture, leather-bound books, architectural drawings and icons, fitting them skillfully to the much larger spaces. "And then I purchased twice as many more pieces," he says. "I really like to mix English, French, Scandinavian and Russian designs, and there are enough rooms here to do that successfully. After years of collecting sixteenth- and seventeenth-century rugs, I finally have places to use them."

The partners enjoy meals and entertain guests in the downstairs room that also serves as Mr. Posey's sitting room. "An area used solely for dining is boring and a waste of space," Mr. Hail explains. "This arrangement works very well for entertaining—cocktails in the living room, then downstairs for dinner in the smaller sitting room. After dinner, guests wander all through the house, as they would in a pavilion. The layout invites it—an aspect I particularly love about the design." Remembering the distinguished architect who first transformed the home, Mr. Hail comments, "I think Julia Morgan would be pleased."

ABOVE: In 1911 architect Julia Morgan added the classic façade to the late-1800s house.

OPPOSITE: The living room plan incorporates the designer's collections of antiques and architectural drawings.

ABOVE: Fond of mixing styles, the designer embellished the downstairs sitting room with an 18th-century French marble mantel, Swedish sconces, circa 1800, and a Russian chandelier. Upholstery fabrics include Danish glove leather and Italian silk velvet. The marble relief portrays Louis XIV.

OPPOSITE: In the sitting room, which doubles as a dining room, the strong background color—a departure for the designer in his own home—and festooned silk shades contribute to the inviting mood. The japanned chinoiserie clock is 18th-century English.

118

"The arrangement brings to mind European households in which generations of a family share the space and maintain private rooms as well."

ABOVE LEFT: *Striped silk unifies Mr. Hail's bedroom. The designer often uses a screen, as in this room, to break the space. The desk is Russian, circa 1785.*

ABOVE RIGHT: *In Mr. Hail's bedroom, gilded Regency chairs are part of a symmetrical arrangement.*

OPPOSITE: *A procession of doorways creates a vista and a free flow of movement from the living room to the opposite end of the house. Painters from Holland treated the doors with eighteen coats of lacquer and varnish.*

Keith B. Irvine

Keith Irvine

"I have always kept close to what I admired when I was a schoolboy; 1840 was my 'moment,' then as now—the Lord Melbourne period, roughly everything from Regency to mid-Victorian."

There was a time when few successful New York interior designers in search of a country house of their own would have been tempted by an American Victorian farmhouse, however unspoiled its setting. Now, however, Keith Irvine's choice of such a house in New England seems almost classic. The British-born designer made his choice about twenty years ago, and that choice might well be described as farsighted. Characteristically, he was less concerned with trend setting than with acquiring a house mellowed by age.

He intended it as a retreat for himself, his wife—at that time also a designer in New York City—and their two daughters. Gradually it became a year-round residence. In addition, the barn has been turned into an alternative house where the Irvines spend the summer, making a seasonal move of a hundred yards.

Rehabilitation and refurnishing over the last fifteen years have been a combined family effort. "We did everything ourselves," Keith Irvine says, "except the electrical work and the plumbing. Almost every piece of furniture has at one time or another been in every room in the house. The living room lace curtains—which we dipped in tea—have been in only three rooms so far, but they will no doubt end up as costumes for one of the masques that we write and perform each year in the garden."

A small part of the farmhouse dates from 1790, but the rest is a typical 1870s construction, with relatively large rooms well suited to the kind of décor—lighthearted and genuinely comfortable—that is second nature to Keith Irvine. Though he is unwilling to take himself too seriously, it would be wrong to assume that this designer is merely an amiable joker; rather, he knows the refinements of his profession so thoroughly that he is able to be somewhat casual about them.

As a young Scot in England in the 1950s, he served for four years as assistant to one of the outstanding masters of twentieth-century interior design, the late John Fowler. Some of the most cherished pieces in Keith Irvine's house today were bequeathed to him by his famous mentor. Of his deeper indebtedness, he says, "John's influence on me was great, but it was largely unconscious. After coming to America, I didn't do anything very 'Fowler' to begin with. I did things that were less grand. But I have been working back to what he taught me."

In his work, Keith Irvine is not limited to re-creating traditional interiors or playing variations on any particular period theme. He has an equally skilled touch with strictly contemporary design. But in Mr. Irvine's own house, there is undeniably much that is pleasantly evocative of the decorative technique in which John Fowler excelled. It is rather easier to list the ingredients than to describe the dish. Superlative English furniture and carefully oiled and preserved leather-bound books, many flowered chintzes, needlework carpets, animal portraits, quilts, a touch of tartan and a twist of Gothic—one and all play their memorable role in the interior of the Irvine farmhouse. So, too, do innumerable less-predictable elements: an Edwardian Chippendale-style table, the throne on which Vivien Leigh sat when she played Cleopatra, a portrait of Mr. Irvine in his youth, wittily disguised as Mary, Queen of Scots.

"I like mixing 1920s and 1930s American rattan with very good classical pieces, Staffordshire china with Chinese Export porcelain," says Keith Irvine. "I started collecting Staffordshire in my boyhood, when you could buy it for seven and sixpence apiece. I stopped only after I bought a Shakespeare statuette that cost $250. For me, Staffordshire has a literary quality that I love."

The same might be said about his own stylistic idiom. Like so much else of British provenance, it is a form of literature once removed. It has sometimes been called "the English-country-house style." It has a lot to do with sound education and a sense of humor, with wood fires and open windows, with buttered toast for tea, with children and with dogs.

*"Almost every piece of furniture
has at one time or another been
in every room in the house."*

*The colonnaded front portico of the 1870s Victorian farm-
house adds distinction to the clapboard structure.*

The robust textures of local stone, rough-hewn beams, and a natural raffia rug establish the rustic appeal of the spacious, hearth-warmed dining room. A mid-Victorian Scottish oil painting of a boy evokes the house's period of origin. The cabin trunk harks back to the same era. Above the mantel is a fantasy portrait by William C. Richards.

In the sitting room, an early-18th-century burl-wood cabinet shelters English porcelain animals. Poised beneath a Chippendale-style mirror, two Staffordshire King Charles spaniels survey a cushioned sofa covered in floral chintz.

Enhancing the traditional look of the dining room is a folding screen covered with early-19th-century wallpaper panels by Jean Züber. Hollyhocks bloom on the drapery chintz.

A child's bedroom abounds in whimsy, as vintage dolls
mingle with contemporary toys. A delicate muslin, fancifully
draped above a 19th-century American bed, combines with
sheer curtains and a pinstripe wallpaper to create a light
and airy setting.

128

An 1860 American mahogany canopy bed dominates a bedroom and anchors the gaiety of Victorian wallpaper, patterned chintz, and bedside table drapery fashioned from a Victorian lace dress.

Sally Sirkin Lewis

*". . . to do something terribly
innovative, and just let my fancy fly
and my imagination go into action."*

"When interior designer Sally Sirkin Lewis and her husband decided to move from their large Beverly Hills home—his four children and her two fledglings were flying on their own by then—she had fixed ideas about what their next house should be. "Don't show me a house that has anything less than a ten-foot ceiling," she told the real estate brokers. "Don't show me a house that doesn't have separate rooms—separate living room, separate dining room, everything separate. Don't show me a house with sliding doors."

That was in 1976, and the house they found, which is currently in the process of being completely rebuilt, had all of the features that the designer disliked. Nevertheless, it had, as she says, "a certain ambience. I can't ever explain it, but there was something I hadn't seen anywhere else."

The décor she evolved was entirely personal: sophisticated, formal, contemporary, a graphic definition of style. Its locale could have been Paris or Milan or New York; it happened to be Beverly Hills, but the design language was international.

The impetus for the design came years ago, at the shop of an antiques dealer in New York. That's where Sally Sirkin Lewis first saw the Japanese screen from which she took the theme that inspired the living room. "For a long time there had been a screen folded up at the shop of one of my antiques dealers, and I had been asking to see it," she says. Finally the dealer did open it, revealing a design with a bird—an Oriental crane—the prototype of those of the flock that would eventually swoop silently around the walls of the Lewis home. Painted directly on soft gold leaf paper, the birds, which were painted by Arthur Fine, circled the living and dining rooms.

The result was riveting, a bold and imaginative statement. Framed by ebony floors and banquettes covered with white Indian cotton, the birds instantly demanded the attention of guests entering the area. The designer explains that she doesn't often indulge her fantasies. "Some people would call them outlandish, but for the first time in my design life, I was able to do something that I didn't have to answer to anybody for."

She had already completed plans for the house: "very Milan, brushed steel walls, brass moldings, geometric carpet, lots of velour, very different from the final result." On thinking things over, however, she said to herself, "That's been done before," and she decided to indulge her flair for drama instead. With this decision came the new plans. "It all happened in one night," she explains. "With the exception of the mantel, I designed everything: the banquettes, the colors, the sisal carpeting, the blinds, the dining room pieces. Everything happened that night, and it was exactly what I wanted. I like to live with a bit of formality. For myself, I don't like an explicitly California 'look.' It's not for me. I don't dress that way; never owned a pair of jeans in my life."

Because the house was small, with one bedroom and a study that doubled as a guest room, the owners made some structural changes, turning windows into glass doors that opened onto the deck they added. And they gave an Oriental feeling to the garden to introduce the mood of the interiors. The black glass lining the walls of the entrance hall gave an immediate cue to the drama within, a drama that played across the designer's mind so strongly that when the room was completed, it contained no shocks, no surprises.

"Although clients are surprised that I'm not excited while an installation is taking place, I know exactly what it's going to look like—exactly. It was the same thing here: there were no disappointments; there was nothing I would have done differently. During the job, though, there was one funny moment: I came in when they had started to lay the gold leaf paper on the walls. It was around noon, so it must have been full sun, and I thought, 'We're all going to be blinded!' This, of course, was before the birds were painted on the walls, a project that started on a much smaller scale—with one bird—and was originally scheduled to be completed in ten days. The job took

> *"For myself, I don't like an explicitly California 'look.' I like to live with a slight bit of formality."*

over four months to finish, which meant that the painter was still hard at it when the carpenters, electricians, carpet installers and furniture movers invaded the premises." "But it was all very calm," the artist, Arthur Fine, remembers. "I would just move to another wall out of the way while they worked. Sally stood there with poise, directing the operation like a symphony conductor."

The finished design suited her well. The soft gold leaf walls echoed her honey-colored hair and complemented her coloring. The pillows heaped on the white banquettes, the black mantel—all provided an ideal background for her. The home was right, too, for the kind of entertaining she prefers. "I entertain only the people I truly enjoy being with. I don't give big parties. But I do like to have people over often—two, four or six. This was a marvelous room for the way we lived. Just four or six of us would have dinner, and then we'd go over to the banquettes and talk until two in the morning. At the time it was just my kind of house. It really was."

Great cranes soar gracefully above the living room banquettes in stylized prominence. The murals, painted by Arthur Fine on gold leaf tea-papered walls, were derived from a Japanese Muromachi screen. A sisal rug adds to the minimal feeling, while faux stone tables add ruggedness.

The dining room continues the innovative look. Antique Japanese lacquer trays reaffirm the bird motif.

Tall period candlesticks illuminate the glass-topped table and Chippendale-style bleached horn chairs.

ABOVE: Crisp white duck complements the twinkling lights of Los Angeles that accompany terrace dining.

OPPOSITE: A geometric-patterned carpet unifies the bold color contrasts in the master bedroom. Lending mystery is an ancient Japanese bronze Buddha.

136

Loyd Ray Taylor *Charles Patton Gremillion, Jr.*

Taylor   Gremillion

"We have mixed château pieces with court pieces, but I don't think any of the craftsmen would be offended."

For designers Loyd Ray Taylor and Charles Paxton Gremillion, Jr., the style of their apartment was determined by its setting—twenty stories above the sparkling lights of Dallas. "We definitely did the apartment as a high rise," explains Mr. Taylor, while Mr. Gremillion points out that the apartment's view is not of the tall buildings of downtown but rather of the residential area that stretches for miles north of the city. At night they look out at millions of lights that seem to extend without end. This spectacular evening panorama is, of course, one of the features the apartment is designed to emphasize.

In the entrance hall, living room and library—which all flow together as one area—the only exterior wall is solid glass from floor to ceiling. All of the interior walls are mirrored; the floors are black marble, and the ceilings have fourteen coats of matte black lacquer. "At night the ceiling and floor seem to disappear, and the mirrored walls reflect the lights," says Mr. Gremillion. "Most places have landmarks, but here there are none. When you are up this high, you could be anyplace in the world. All you can see are lights and stars."

The two designers are native Texans and have been partners since 1960. In some ways the apartment is almost an extension of their shop, which specializes in fine antiques, since through the years they have kept exceptional pieces for their personal collection. A noteworthy example is a magnificent Louis XV desk of parqueted tulipwood signed by Mathieu Criaerd, a major court cabinetmaker. The desk, which is a focal point in the library, features an intricate locking mechanism, a number of concealed compartments and elaborate gilt-bronze ornamentation. They feel great affection for such examples of fine workmanship. "The man who made that desk actually put his life into it and created a work of art," says Mr. Taylor. "Through the years, a piece like this one has been bought and cared for by people who love quality. Such a piece of furniture has gone through many hands before it reaches us, and it will go through many more after we are gone."

Their previous apartment had a different arrangement, so in planning their move, they had to dispose of several of their favorite pieces. "Because this apartment can't take a lot of furniture, it forced us to be very selective. A collector is forced to refine and distill if he is going to build a proper collection."

They agree that one of their goals in designing the apartment about eight years ago was to "create an environment that draws attention to the furnishings, not to wall surfaces or fabrics. We wanted the walls to float, so that pieces of furniture would stand out like pieces of sculpture or other works of art." The dark mirrored walls, which provide that muted floating background, have been accented by a platinum band; "we didn't want to use architectural paneling, but we did want a suggestion of molding—a feeling that something is here, though it doesn't quite exist."

There are no coverings on the windows in the living room, library and entrance hall, and the upholstery is tooled leather. "It's rather refreshing to use no fabric for a change. When we tell people that the apartment is all lacquer, leather, mirrors and marble, they think it's Art Déco. It's not. It's really a kind of fantasy."

The owners consider the apartment very personal and intimate, because it concentrates on furnishings, art objects and books they have collected over a number of years. While many of the pieces are eighteenth- or early-nineteenth-century French, the apartment is by no means in one period style. In the living room, for example, a handsome twelve-panel Chinese screen, presented to a noblewoman on her sixtieth birthday in 1715, extends across an entire wall. The same room also holds a Regency récamier, a Russian table, an Italian console and eight chairs from a set made by Georges Jacob for the Empress Josephine's retreat, *Malmaison*. Mr. Taylor and

Mr. Gremillion use four of the eight chairs at the white marble and gilt table in the center of the living room and scatter the others throughout the room. "Then we can pull the other chairs up to the table when we have guests. A center table is very European; it makes the room a salon."

Accessories and art objects in the library also testify to the owners' wide-ranging tastes. Ornate French clocks, Art Déco boxes by Cartier, a pair of eighteenth-century Swedish candelabra made of lapis, a jeweled silver box from Germany, a Fabergé hippopotamus carved from jade, and lamps made from Chinese porcelains mounted in bronze join an impressive bronze equestrian statue of Louis XIV. The original statue, which weighed about thirty tons, has been destroyed, but the artist, Girardon, made and signed a number of reductions, this among them.

The owners have also collected antique, one-of-a-kind table and bar accessories and serving pieces. They enjoy setting out the gilt, vermeil, mother-of-pearl and crystal pieces they have acquired at formal dinner parties for fourteen, setting one round table for seven in the living room and another in the entrance hall. They like people to recognize that it is possible to entertain formally in an apartment without a formal dining room. For dinner parties the partners use masses of flowers everywhere, preferably ivory roses or ivory gladiolus. And they like to have music so that guests can dance in the entrance hall. "We like to have a harp and a flute for some parties," says Mr. Gremillion. "Both seem to fit the mood of the apartment exactly."

In the main living area, objects are set off in space against the dark background. A well-ordered arrangement includes a Régence commode, a leather-covered Régence fauteuil, a Louis XV bracket clock and a Louis Philippe giltwood taboret. Bouquets of roses and lighted candles add drama.

141

"When you are up this high, you could be anyplace in the world. All you can see are lights and stars."

Formal dinners are served in the living room, which is enhanced by the glittering gold-leaf decoration on the set of leather-covered armchairs by Jacob and by sparkling cut crystal table garniture. Antique porcelains and two Chinese lacquer screens contribute Oriental overtones, while a lacquered ceiling amplifies the hard-surface luster of marble flooring. A ribbon-trimmed moiré tablecloth adds sheen.

143

ABOVE LEFT: The library features a late Ch'ien Lung painting on silk and a Louis XV secrétaire à dessus brisé signed by Criaerd; the drop front holds crystal hand seals and gemstone-set Russian writing accoutrements.

LEFT AND OPPOSITE: A bedroom/sitting room displays a matched set of 18th-century Chinese silk embroideries, a pair of rare 16th-century Indian marble figures on an Italian commode, and four Louis XVI transitional fauteuils signed Carpentier. Light-hued bed linens are enclosed by dark bed draperies.

Anthony Machado (signature)

Anthony Machado

*"Moving something from one position
to another can completely transform
one's sense of place, as well as the
particular objects in it."*

Today's urban residents are having to adjust to compact environments as the large homes of the nineteenth and early twentieth centuries are supplanted by far smaller spaces. The San Francisco apartment where interior designer Anthony Machado lived for several years, before his move to Los Angeles in 1981, was in a high-rise building on Nob Hill with panoramic views of the city. The apartment itself was small, with three rooms, none of them particularly large or distinguished; yet Mr. Machado decided to re-create the drama of a palace within this limited space.

He achieved a sense of mystery and grandeur in the small quarters by establishing guidelines that were followed throughout the design. The backgrounds of walls, floors and ceilings were subdued in black or soft natural tones of beige or gold. The sofas and side tables in the living room, for example, were simply styled and subtly colored to enhance the lavish display of objects in the foreground, which were compelling focal points that enriched the spatial experience.

The living room exhibited a variety of objects, the most dazzling being a bronze sculpture from 1920 by Wilhelm Lehmbruck. Its presence was reflected in the opposite corner of the room by colossal twin mirrored screens. The six-foot-high Lucite frames designed by Mr. Machado were backlighted, the mirrors inside them dramatically reflecting the objects and furnishings in cubistic compositions of contoured and angular forms. At night each object was lighted from behind or spotlighted from above, thereby appearing to glow from within. Reflections from surrounding surfaces had an effect that was both majestic and magical. Quilted black vinyl shades covered the windows and echoed the ribbed ceiling above. Originally raw concrete, the ceiling was painted a high-gloss black. Light sparkled everywhere. Brazilian topaz quartz coals in the fireplace were lighted from behind and radiated dramatically through a tempered glass screen.

Mr. Machado believes that "the spectator appreciates art best if he can participate in placing it in different perspectives to achieve renewed vitality"; so he often moved his collection of artworks, objects and furnishings around to experience more fully their subtle characters and changing qualities. The designer also used lighting to enhance this sense of energy, for it can pinpoint one aspect of an object or it can be adjusted to underline some area within a room.

Consider, for example, the small—twelve by fifteen feet—bedroom the designer transformed into a regal space. Walls were upholstered with cotton sewn horizontally, which created lines that extended into the mirrored surfaces on the side walls and the window covering. The room seemed built from large slabs of stone stacked horizontally. The reflective gold-foil ceiling increased the apparent height of the room, and twin mirrors opposite one another on the side walls extended the sensation of depth.

The centerpiece was, of course, the bed, which Mr. Machado thought of as his "spacecraft," a self-contained unit that seemed to hover above the floor. The designer achieved this effect by recessing the base, mirroring the recess, and concealing lighting underneath. This lighting was, in fact, the only major source of illumination in the room. It accented the soft texture of the quilted walls and carpeted floors and could be seen in the mirrors and ceiling above. A Mongolian royal guardsman's uniform covered a wall behind the bed, and the foil ceiling echoed the richly embroidered golden uniform.

The designer collected many of the objects in the apartment during his travels, and they represent historically more than a thousand years of artistic invention. By integrating such objects into a space shaped by his sense of the dramatic, Mr. Machado was able to transform the several small and undistinguished rooms of the San Francisco apartment into a gallery that celebrated the palatial splendor of the past and alluded to the challenge and mystery of the future.

ABOVE: *The entrance hall heralds a mise-en-scène of mystery and grandeur. Japanese porcelains mingle with 19th-century screens while shadows reflect on walls and floor.*

RIGHT: *Lighting wizardry enhances the dark, glistening surfaces and muted earth tones of the living room. Soaring like light-edged skyscrapers, mirrored screens echo Mr. Machado's granite sphere sculpture.*

FOLLOWING PAGES: *Cambodian temple dogs guard the passage to the dining room, where the table becomes a stage for a grandiloquent samurai. Gold leaf paper covers the ceiling, an aureate plane afloat in the darkness.*

"The spectator appreciates art best if he can participate in placing it in different perspectives to achieve renewed vitality."

A spherical sculpture by Pomodoro and a Mongolian palace guard's uniform proclaim an exotic order in the master bedroom. The shimmering ceiling reflects infinitely, while the bed, which includes an audiovisual control center, appears to hover above a field of light. Quilted bedcovering and wall upholstery are a soft foil for the hard-surface gleam.

Robert Metzger

"You really have to be very economical with the disposition of pieces in a room, just as a writer, even a very lyrical writer, must be absolutely clear about his choice of words. He can't say violet if he means mauve."

In a period of great mobility it is highly unusual to find anyone in Manhattan who has lived in the same apartment for thirty years. What makes this particular instance still more surprising is that the person in question is Robert Metzger. As an interior designer, he belongs to a profession that thrives on change—on the reworking of space and the rearrangement of objects.

Such activities usually entail a change of address, but Mr. Metzger remains happily ensconced in a solid prewar building on Central Park West. His apartment is a visual feast of colors and shapes in a mixture of periods and styles. Under Mr. Metzger's skillful baton, the décor becomes a celebration of the pleasures of surface and form, and beneath the more incandescent qualities is a sense of control, even sobriety.

"The apartment has been through at least five major transformations over the years, but I've never made any major architectural alterations," says the designer. "The changes have always been a matter of new furniture, paint, new objects—things that are more or less ephemeral." This sense of continuity gives the richly colored rooms, with their whirl of individual elements, an undertone of calm and assurance.

"The design didn't all happen yesterday," says Robert Metzger. "That much is obvious. It's been an incremental thing, shaped by comfort and by practicality. You know, when you're actually living in an apartment, you're less tempted to undertake sweeping architectural changes." The designer believes that limitations such as this one benefit design. "Whether it's the fact that you can't bear to live for months with the dust and debris of demolition or whether it's the particular needs of the clients, having a limit of some kind helps you be more ingenious."

With a keen eye for the unusual or the unsung, the designer comments, "I can always find a home for something I love." The objects of his affections include virtually anything made of shagreen;

Indo-Portuguese furniture of precious materials; smoothly elegant pieces of Art Déco—in fact, anything that suggests the marriage of the delicate and the robust that has become his hallmark.

"I hesitate to bring clients here, though," he says, "not because I am an especially private person; it's just that I don't think my solutions for my own home would necessarily apply to anyone else. To me this is a 'personality' apartment—*my* personality. I couldn't duplicate it for someone else. It's also a kind of autobiography; a good apartment always is. I remember exactly when and where I bought every piece. I have to have good feelings about anything I own and about the circumstances in which I acquired it."

Mood is an important word in Mr. Metzger's vocabulary. "I use color to create it," he explains. "Color unifies a room and gives it a glow. Then there are the things to avoid: No period fabrics for me, or old brocades. I don't like mustiness. I try for fresh, sparkling rooms. We're living in the eighties, a fabulous era, so let's look like it." Ruffles are another interdiction. "Strong, clear-cut shapes are important to me. Just as I like strong personalities, I'm attracted to bold shapes. Nothing bland or fuzzy."

Throughout the apartment the ambience is full-blooded and complex, never stifling or cloying. An almost astringent editorial instinct is at work. "Function, that's the explanation," says Mr. Metzger. "Every object has to give something, even if it's sheer, outrageous beauty. That's where selectivity comes in."

It is this underlying sense of purpose that makes the apartment appear so effortless in spite of its overtones of opulence. Discipline and a slow and careful shifting about of objects over time can only result from a stable and ongoing relationship with a living space. Robert Metzger has reaped this reward from his long and happy tenancy on Central Park West.

*"To me this is a 'personality'
apartment—my personality.
I couldn't duplicate it for
someone else."*

*ABOVE: In the entrance hall, an adroit composition
includes a Japanese chest and a contemporary brass-
framed mirror. The watercolor is by Henry Moore. The dark
background, upholstered in stamped velvet, serves to
expand the compact space.*

*OPPOSITE: The cock of the walk—or of the living room—
is a 19th-century gilt example. The palette used here illustrates the designer's belief that color can unify a space
and make it glow. The painting is Léger's* Paysage, 1932.

*FOLLOWING PAGES: Seating runs the stylistic gamut in
the living room, from a pair of Régence bergères to a contemporary chaise longue to a Ch'ing Dynasty audience
chair. The window treatment combines lacquered vertical
wooden shutters with balloon shades and chinoiserie
upholstered screens—these last echoed by a Chinese coromandel screen.*

156

ABOVE: *The combined library/dining room deftly bridges varied functions in a small compass. A contemporary handkerchief table opens to a square, capable of seating eight to maximize flexibility. The bronze-mirrored wall visually amplifies the room. Reflected in it are a pair of 18th-century figurative pedestals flanking a painting by James Harvard. The pair of 18th-century doors made into a cabinet enclose a television set and stereo equipment.*

OPPOSITE: *Walls covered in ceiling tin make the master bedroom a gleaming nighttime world. The Art Déco desk of shagreen and wood and the bench are signed Dominique. The round plate is Japanese cloisonné. The kitelike construction, titled Muybridge, is by Richard Smith.*

160

Joe Minton *David Corley*

Joseph Minton   David Corley

"When we work on a project, we can't really separate ideas and point out what each of us contributed individually. Often we think of the very same thing."

After fifteen years in business together, interior designers Joseph Minton and David Corley of Fort Worth, Texas, consider their tastes almost identical. "We work so well together," says Mr. Minton, "that we need very little conversation. David can answer a question before I've even finished asking it, because he knows what I'm going to say."

This smooth teamwork has been the characteristic of the firm of Minton-Corley since 1969, although the designers have known each other since college days. At first, however, each pursued a separate career, David Corley entering the field of interior design, Joseph Minton becoming a lawyer and later vice-president of a bank. Coincidentally, when the bank decided to redecorate its executive offices and make a number of changes in its lobby, Mr. Minton was the staff member assigned to work with the Corley design firm on the project. Their ideas meshed happily, and they decided to join forces.

They do not feel that they have one particular style, and they enjoy working with the décor of any period, whether traditional or contemporary. This versatility of interest is essential, in fact, since the range of their projects includes Texas ranch houses as well as apartments in Paris.

Perhaps the design element they emphasize most is lighting. "As a matter of fact, we've been known to tear out the entire ceiling of a two-story house when it wasn't possible to install the proper lighting from above," says Mr. Corley. "And remember that you can't sit in your office during the day and design room lighting on paper. You have to be there in the room itself after dark to work on it—the entire character of a room changes at night." They stress the importance of "letting a room glow" and of keeping the light source hidden. For this reason they prefer lights recessed in the ceiling or uplighting behind plants.

Although their tastes are strikingly similar, it is interesting to find that their approach to the décor of their own residences was far from identical—in spite of the fact that they collaborated on one another's homes. "Naturally, we like many of the same decorative elements," says Mr. Corley; "but of course, there are different things each of us prefers to live with." In Mr. Minton's former home, for example, there were many Oriental pieces, including a collection of porcelain vases. Contrastingly, the Corleys have gathered together more primitive art objects—Apache baskets and a ceremonial costume from New Guinea. They also have examples of Greek and Roman pottery.

Mr. Minton lived in his former home for something more than nine years. The designer recalls that he wanted to buy it from the moment he set eyes on the eleven-foot ceilings. Over the years, of course, much work was done on the house. Some of the paneling was replaced, and the library/sitting room was redesigned to complement the adjacent master bedroom. On the other side of the bedroom was a handsome and comfortable dressing suite separated into two sections by a plant-filled atrium with skylights.

Other renovations were necessary as well, many of them required by the fact that Joseph Minton does a great deal of entertaining. "In the beginning," he explains, "I used the library as the sitting room, but I found that since I much preferred it to the living room, I ended up doing a good deal of entertaining there. It really wasn't large enough, so I decided to change the living room to an area reserved more or less exclusively for parties. It definitely seemed that it would be a 'night' room at first, but it was just as effective during the day; so I found myself using the new living room even when I didn't have guests." One of the most handsome pieces of furniture in the room was a sixteenth-century Dutch cabinet, which David Corley found many years ago at the Metro-Goldwyn-Mayer auction in California.

Mr. Corley's own home is on a hill overlooking the Trinity River valley, surrounded by trees and with a lovely view enhanced by more than two hundred azalea bushes. The location of the house dictated some immediate changes when

"No matter how beautiful a room is during the day, it won't be effective at night without the correct lighting."

the Corleys first moved in about ten years ago. Many of the windows were enlarged to take advantage of the view, and special shades were devised to cut down on the glare. The family's size demanded a functional interior, and the den—filled with casual Italian wicker furniture—was set aside primarily for use by the children.

The house is comfortable and efficient for a large family, a fact that can be seen particularly in the dining room and in the kitchen. The dining room table has a massive glass top supported by sections of two large tree trunks. The designer redid the kitchen entirely. A raised ceiling and skylights make the room seem even larger.

Both Joseph Minton's former home and David Corley's present home suggest an intriguing paradox. While the same basic design elements were used in each home, the results were quite as different as they were similar, each being suited to the needs of the particular designer. Considered side by side, the similarities and differences suggest at once the versatility and the individuality of the men who head the firm of Minton-Corley. The houses were far from identical although both interiors could have been designed by the same hand. And in a curious way, they were.

The Minton Residence

ABOVE: An intriguing collection of ivory animals is displayed on an English Georgian tilt-top table.

OPPOSITE: In the living room, deft lighting, deep tones and a geometric-patterned carpet create drama. The mirror is Venetian; the crystal sconces date from the 18th century. French crystal pieces cluster on the tabletop.

The Corley Residence

OPPOSITE: A skylighted atrium separates dressing areas in the Minton master bedroom suite.

ABOVE: An original and exotic flavor pervades David Corley's living room. Palms and cacti punctuate the warm-toned space, which is enlivened by diverse patterns. The painting is by James R. Blake.

167

ABOVE LEFT AND ABOVE RIGHT: Lending mystery to the living room are such primitive objects as a suspension hook and woven dance costume from New Guinea; Apache baskets, and an Ashanti wooden doll.

OPPOSITE: The sunroom leads to a spacious terrace.

Lee Radziwill

Lee Radziwill

"I don't belong to the school of interior design that believes in effacing the past every five years."

Simplicity is a happy condition in interior design, and one that is not always easily attainable. Carried to an extreme, it can verge on the bleak or, when not taken far enough, appears merely inconclusive. A simple arrangement must be both fresh and unaffected if it is to create the critical illusion of artlessness. In the airy suite of rooms that were Lee Radziwill's home before she moved into a New York townhouse, these conditions were particularly well met.

The penthouse of a classic New York building, the apartment was a fascinating mix of the past and a light-filled, informal present. "When I moved there from my previous apartment, two blocks away, it represented the opening up of my life to clarity and simplicity. I did take some pieces with me, but I was selective, because the demands of a penthouse are obviously quite different from those of a duplex. Here one of my first decisions was to make everything extremely flexible and easy. An important step was the choice of wooden shutters rather than draperies throughout the apartment. The unaffected quality of the shutters and the quality of the light as it streamed in set the mood for the whole space, I think." And indeed it did. For although they may have delineated the outlines of a Louis XVI Jacob chair, the morning light and the golden afternoon haze discreetly softened its urbane sumptuousness.

A terrace, wrapped around the entire perimeter of the apartment, inspired the designer to plan a richly evocative garden. "I chose blue, silver and white plants, which created a wonderfully soft aura of color when viewed from within the apartment." This floral theme was pursued indoors as well, and handpainted silk blossoms appeared on sofa pillows. Floral wallcovering and upholstery added their notes, while underfoot, the Bessarabian rug in the living room lent its own commentary to this festival of flowers. "I suppose I wanted to lull myself into thinking I was in the English countryside," says the designer.

Yet a cosmopolitan accent was also quite persistent in these rooms, whether in the elegant curves of the Regency dining chairs with their hocked legs or in the conscious sentimentality of the Landseer paintings, embodying as they do a particularly Victorian vision of innocence. Although the apartment itself was simple, the way of life it suggested was quite sophisticated.

The true spirit of the apartment could best be detected in one of Mrs. Radziwill's few concessions to formality. In the reception room, she installed wainscoting around the walls. It was a particularly delicate and precise gesture, one that served to delineate the room and, at the same time, to establish its scale and to place it within a disciplined context.

She was concerned throughout with what she describes as "subtle, old-fashioned virtues. An escape from the harsh present into a softer, more gentle way of life, an opening up to light and the weather. When you have a garden," she observes, "you're constantly aware of the seasons; it's a sense of real luxury. By this I mean the kind of luxury that cannot be measured by monetary standards—a level of tranquillity, a sweetness of tone, an uncomplicated background for the ongoing complexity of life." It is precisely this balance of simplicity and ambiguity that Lee Radziwill achieved in her Manhattan apartment.

LEFT AND ABOVE: In the living room and throughout the apartment, wooden shutters were chosen for the soft filtered light they admit. Comfortable upholstered seating reinforces the mood of understatement, which is subtly tempered by antique pieces: a pair of Louis XVI chairs by Jacob, Louis XVI marquetry tables, a bouillotte lamp with tôle shade and an Empire urn made into a lamp. A Bessarabian rug anchors the arrangement, while the addition of wainscoting strengthens the architectural symmetry of the room. Paintings by James Ward represent a 19th-century aesthetic, and a Roman head evokes antiquity.

173

While maintaining the informal tone of the décor, the dining room presents a more highly stylized setting. Here the floral leitmotiv—evident in the 19th-century botanical prints, the wallcovering and the Bessarabian rug—is countered by classically inspired furnishings: A Greek key motif adorns the Regency cabinet, and the rosewood dining table, from the same era, rests on a base of gilded dolphins. Regency armchairs complete the balanced ensemble.

174

"I suppose I wanted to lull myself into thinking I was in the English countryside."

In the master bedroom, painted wood appointments, a light-hued rug and stenciled flooring extend the airy feeling characteristic of the décor. A witty effect, the upholstered steps placed at the foot of the bed emphasize the height of the early-19th-century English four-poster. A delicately painted Victorian clock tolls the hours above an 18th-century Austrian desk, which is accompanied by an English wheel-back chair. The distinctive Louis XVI lyre-back chair was designed to facilitate conversation.

177

[signature: Valerian S. Rybar]

Valerian Rybar

"You need architecture to make good rooms.
It gives you discipline, nobility, beauty."

Creating a truly successful fantasy world within a contemporary New York apartment is one of the most difficult of all feats to achieve. First of all, there are the almost inflexible confines of postwar buildings' dimensions. Then there is an almost equally important psychological barrier to overcome: It can be disconcerting to enter a space in which boundaries seem to melt away, in which day becomes night. To do this and still not cross the fine line between the simply magical and the meretriciously bizarre is the special province of Valerian Rybar.

"My home is, of course, a highly personal environment," says the designer. "I was pleasing no one but myself and a few special friends. To me this is the ideal situation. One can experiment with unusual materials and effects without having to worry about a frantic phone call from a client, who, for example, might dislike the lighting system. In addition, I have very particular—even idiosyncratic—tastes, and I certainly don't think this apartment is for everyone. It is a very richly figured little universe I've created here. Naturally, it's highly specialized."

When Mr. Rybar originally chose the apartment, he planned it down to the last detail, and he has found no need to make any major changes since. "Of course I've added pieces, but essentially the apartment is as it was ten years ago."

By Manhattan standards, it is in a perfect location, in the Sutton Place area, and it possesses that rare quality, a door that opens directly onto the street. As a result, it has a curiously intimate air. It is a delightful arrangement, which the designer wishes were more common in New York.

To enter the apartment, especially at night, is to be handed a visa to a delectable jeweled world. Lighting suggests untold luxuries of surface, as spots pick out unique objects and humble pieces alike. Valerian Rybar is supremely democratic in his choice of accessories. Simple wooden toys from Mexico rub shoulders with intricate objects that could have originated in the *Kunst-*

kammer of a central European prince. Yet it is democracy filtered through an aristocratic sensibility, for all the objects possess the mark of Mr. Rybar's taste: a fascination with the mysterious, the half revealed. Many of his pieces are anecdotal, exotic figments of elaborate scenarios hinting at narratives that can only be guessed.

A coolly considered organization of the space prevents this plethora of detail from ever becoming oppressive. The apartment falls naturally into two separate zones, a public and a private. The first three rooms are the public spaces, which are collectively a tour de force. On the right as the apartment is entered is a living room in rich warm tones. On the left is a more intimate living room intended for smaller gatherings. Connecting the two is a bold touch, the witty "library," in which all of the books are actually only bindings; they have startling titles and suggest a mock biography of the designer himself. A second layer of rooms behind these three constitute the private realm. Colors become darker, and the mood is introspective. These interiors present the more austere face of this world of fantasy.

At the time Mr. Rybar took the apartment, he was rebelling against the prevailing style of interior design. "I think we were all tired of white walls and oversize pieces of art stranded in bare rooms," he says. "I wanted a feeling of sybaritic well-being that would not be sterile." At the same time, the designer experimented with such effects as a textured stainless-steel floor and metal vertical blinds. These items and the many custom-designed pieces of chrome hardware provide a cooling function, preventing the more opulent elements of the rooms from establishing too extravagant a tone.

Many of the designer's ideas, such as tortoiseshell for paneling and stainless-steel moldings, have, to his pleasure, influenced the course of contemporary interior design. "Again, I was experimenting—my brushed stainless-steel tub, for example. Some of the experts I asked told me

the water would get cold instantly; others insisted it would become scalding hot. In the end, it behaved like any other bath water! I played with a lot of ideas and created effects that I have remained very happy with."

At the core of Valerian Rybar's beliefs about interiors is a profound dedication to architecture. Certainly the lively pursuit of fantasy and experimentation—and a response to good architecture—make his residence a bold statement.

Metallic surfaces unify the living room, an opulent cocoon whose vibrant velvet-upholstered walls have rounded corners. The textured steel floor and fireplace surround find sleek complements in the stainless-steel fireplace with concealed lighting, as well as in vertical blinds, moldings and window trim. Low tables are of stainless steel; the beehive-shaped table is of polished steel and Lucite, and the poufs, upholstered in a steel-hued satin, have steel bases.

180

"I have very particular—even idiosyncratic—tastes, and I certainly don't think this apartment is for everyone."

ABOVE: Classic and surrealistic elements coexist in a corner of the living room appointed with a tufted chair and ottoman. The antique bouillotte lamp is accompanied by a stylized painting of a rooster, an 18th-century Bavarian polychrome wooden skeleton and a ceramic version of Salvador Dalí's famous soft watch. In the foreground: a 16th-century German falcon.

OPPOSITE: Humor enlivens the apparently formal dining room, a faux library, in which leather bookbindings are tooled in gold and carry facetious titles alluding to phases in the designer's life. Mirrored panels amplify the space, multiplying the room's two tables, and conceal storage for dinnerware. Surveying the scene is an early marble bust of a Roman emperor that heightens the wit of the setting.

ABOVE: In the master bath, a sybaritic mirrored fantasy, the tub is made of sandblasted steel and the freestanding basin of marble rimmed in steel. On the wall behind the tub is a series of leather-masked wooden heads by Nancy Grossman; they are suspended from chrome-plated metal bars and meat hooks.

OPPOSITE: The master bedroom is dark and mysterious. Flanking the bed are a pair of 16th-century Spanish bishops; above it is a wall sculpture that Mr. Rybar designed and had fabricated in bronze.

Jay Spectre

"This is my statement, and it's my heart on the line. What you are seeing is Jay Spectre, and what I bring to this party is my own individualism, both as a person and as a designer."

"For me, designing a new space is like an opening night on Broadway. There's the excitement, the joy, the anxiety and the frustration all rolled into one," says Jay Spectre. Recently the interior designer had the opportunity to experience this excitement in a very personal way when he created his own home, a relatively small yet richly utilized apartment on Manhattan's Fifth Avenue.

Situated on the eighth floor of a gracious pre–World War II building, the apartment offers a view that extends across Central Park to encompass the skyline of the West Side—a view that Jay Spectre has framed and celebrated by way of a sumptuously designed window seat. Indeed, the expanse of sky and a sunset are as much a part of the apartment's mood as are the furnishings that lend the space its sense of repose.

When John Ruskin stated that "taste is the only morality. . . . Tell me what you like, and I'll tell you what you are," he expressed a credo the designer shares; it holds that an environment always mirrors the person within it. "Aesthetic integrity is what I strive for," Mr. Spectre declares; "whether designing for others or for myself, that is the key issue. What I have conceived for this apartment is a classic twentieth-century design with an emphasis on things Oriental. The reason I love the Orient and Oriental art is because they represent a culture that has survived, flourished, vanished and reemerged. There is a quality of timelessness. For me, just standing in a garden in Kyoto is about as close to heaven as a human being can be on earth. The Far East has always exerted a strong hold on me; I think it has to do with responding to forces beyond our knowledge."

If Jay Spectre's sensibilities draw him to the meditative resonance of the East, he is not unmindful of the equally civilizing pleasures of international style. While the design components of his apartment include superb Japanese and Chinese objects and furnishings, the understated elegance of the space is enhanced by the frankly contemporary accoutrements of comfortable living. The amalgam of generous sofas and armchairs; immaculate glass and steel tables; bleached oak floors and walls; subtly theatrical lighting, and the many twentieth-century paintings, drawings, prints and sculptures attest to the designer's long-standing belief that combinations of fine work of different periods can convey a vibrant oneness.

This achievement of aesthetic balance and symmetry through a confluence of disparate elements is seen in the circular dining room, whose tranquillity and physical well-being combine with unexpected visual pleasures. From the wall cabinet in which is displayed a collection of vases, to Barbara Hepworth's bold circular abstraction, to Mr. Spectre's own round marble-topped table, the room is a lesson in curvilinear articulation. Even the nineteenth-century Japanese screens and the ceiling, painted with Oriental motifs of clouds and water, bear out this geometric emphasis.

"In design, it is important to have a point of view," Mr. Spectre comments, "and a point of view is derived from a sense of style. Style, in turn, comes from an awareness of the world around us. I am influenced by every situation—from the weather, to politics, to economics, to history. My sense of style and taste developed out of a desire to know how people live. I wanted something that would take me where I had never been.

"I do not like being labeled," Mr. Spectre says decisively. "Neither do I like being called a 'modern' designer. I respect any form of design that has been well thought out, well executed and clearly defined. Clarity and integrity are the characteristics that really count.

"Of course, it's extremely difficult to draw the line between my privacy and what I want the public to perceive about me. Once this interior is seen by others, it becomes public knowledge and no longer exists as a purely private statement. Still, this apartment is very much a part of my life, and its design and contents are a part of how I feel and how I think. It gives me that most essential quality—peace of mind."

"This apartment is very much a part of my life, and its design and contents are a part of how I feel and how I think."

LEFT: In the entrance hall, a festive grouping combines a Diego Giacometti table, two of that artist's cat figures and a Germaine Derbecq painting.

OPPOSITE AND FOLLOWING PAGES: Walls covered in hand-woven Chinese raw silk, flooring and window seat of bleached oak, and leather upholstery establish the palette of the living room—a muted foil for a personally expressive mix of art and objects. The painting on the mirrored wall is by Auguste Herbin, and among the artworks reflected are a delicate Cocteau drawing and a painting by Andrée Lucienne Boland. On the table before the sofa rests a Jean Arp sculpture titled Torso-Bird (1963). The Japanese table bears a Diego Giacometti lamp and a pair of Chinese vases.

ABOVE: *Adding interest to the dining room is its circular shape, emphasized by bleached oak molding with steel inserts, and echoed by the marble-topped table. The rounded chairs, by Ruhlmann, are covered in leather. Other enticements: a handpainted canvas ceiling and a wall cabinet displaying a collection of vases. A Tiffany bowl of favrile glass adorns the dining table, on which two Diego Giacometti birds are perched.*

RIGHT: *A corner of the master bedroom was sacrificed to accommodate the circular shape of the dining room; in the process, the bedroom, too, acquired a more distinctive form. The harmonious color scheme of the décor persists, enhanced by a loam-hued carpet. Oriental accents include an Edo period screen, over the bed, and a small Chinese coromandel screen, on the desk. The sculpture is by Raul Valdivieso. The table near the leather-upholstered chair is French Art Déco; the small chair at the desk is of similar vintage. At the foot of the bed is a lacquered trunk that conceals a television set, which emerges hydraulically.*

Leonard W. Stanley

Leonard Stanley

"I don't buy things to put in one particular place. I simply buy what appeals to me, and then I find a place for it."

Pine trees abound, the atmosphere is rustic, and the house calls to mind some happily converted New England barn. It is difficult to realize that Sunset Boulevard lies less than a mile below, where the vast urban expanse of Los Angeles encroaches. When interior designer Leonard Stanley came upon this bucolic retreat more than a decade ago, he knew that he had found the house he wanted.

"It's not to every taste," says the designer. "The place is rather small, and it's rather different." Steep wooden steps lead precipitously up to the entrance of the hilltop house. The door opens, and indeed, the interior is dramatically different. "Do you know what one of my friends said?" laughs Mr. Stanley. "He said the house looks like a barn on the outside and exactly like the pillaging of Peking on the inside!"

The description serves admirably to sum up the essence of the home, one of compelling paradox and immense delight. Leonard Stanley has two major interests in life—designing and collecting—and they both find expression within the confines of this deceptively rustic hillside home. It is an estimable approach to interior décor and an homage to the art of collecting.

The interior is a cornucopia of treasures and oddities spilling outward in every direction. Stately eighteenth-century French antiques share the focus of attention with primitive artifacts from the South Pacific. At first glance, the interior is an extravagant blur of tapestries, paintings, boiseries, crystal chandeliers, plants and—in towering stacks—books, books, books. Leonard Stanley is more than an avid collector; it would seem that he has a veritable mania for collecting—but it is a mania pursued with great good humor and a sense of comforting proportion.

The range of Mr. Stanley's enthusiasms and interests makes the word *eclectic* sound restrictive. One of his favorite possessions is a large seventeenth-century Italian tapestry. "I have to be honest," confides the designer. "I really think I bought the house because it had a wall large enough for my tapestry. But that's a special case. Everything else just seems to fit, one way or another." The extent of "everything else" is impressive. Most striking perhaps are the variety of fabrics and materials used and the range of the art and periods represented. All manner of wood is found throughout the house: eighteenth-century French boiseries, Chinese carved figures, Moroccan grilles and coromandel screens are a few examples. Fabrics suggest a myriad of cultures; they range from Samoan tapa cloth, antique American quilts and Portuguese needlepoint rugs to old Persian materials and African raffia. Objects, too, come from every part of the world: Shaker baskets, semiprecious stone eggs, Greek worry beads, a cane from Barbados made of fish vertebrae are some among a great many others. The art covers as wide a range, from Chinese ancestor portraits to an eighteenth-century painting of Maria Teresa, from watercolors and drawings by Fleur Cowles, Yves Saint Laurent, Ludwig Bemelmans and Cecil Beaton to pictures of Ernest Hemingway in Idaho and photographic studies by Leonard Stanley himself.

There is a profusion of other objects, some of considerable value—but all are of importance to the collector: Mexican madonnas, Egyptian stone carvings, dried leis from Hawaii, shell boxes, oversize pussy willows, statues of Kuan Yin, a collection of Oceanic spears, stuffed animals—the list is endless. "Most people feel it's a little too cluttered," the designer says, with conscious understatement. "But I'm convinced you can have a very busy room without having it look cluttered. That's certainly what I've tried to do here—though I do think the question is academic, since I certainly don't expect people to live the way I do. It's all very personal." Perhaps Mr. Stanley's home is best understood as generous rather than cluttered; after all, his is a unique statement.

However individual and idiosyncratic his own home may be, the designer has firm ideas about interior décor and his professional responsibilities. His clear understanding of scale relationships, for example, is everywhere evident. This can be seen in the skill with which he solved the problem of the small library by manipulating space and reconciling conflicting elements. The room is basically minute, but Mr. Stanley has filled it with very large furniture. In a paradoxical way, the use of such overscale pieces serves to enlarge the sense of space rather than diminish it.

Leonard Stanley is equally at home with traditional or contemporary décor. "I'm very much on the side of the client," he says. "I like the people for whom I'm working to have strong and definite ideas. I suppose it is acceptable for a designer to have trademarks, but I do feel that when you walk into a house, the initial impact should come from the personality of the owner—not the designer." When it comes to this designer's own Los Angeles home, there is no question of identification. The use of space, the careful control, the generous profusion of objects are personal. It is obviously and strikingly a Leonard Stanley interior.

ABOVE AND OPPOSITE: Prominent features of the living room include a French trophy panel above the fireplace, a 17th-century tapestry and two Kuan Yin statues.

OPPOSITE ABOVE: The designer's tendency to use over-scale elements is evident in the 18th-century Chinese porcelain vase in the living room. A playful example of the same tendency is the crayonlike candle next to the vase.

OPPOSITE BELOW: The pine-paneled kitchen is cheerfully bedecked with artworks and flowering plants.

LEFT: Tall 18th-century French château doors lead from the living room to the luxuriantly planted terrace. Ceiling beams and the large-paned window serve as clues to the paradoxically barnlike exterior.

ABOVE: A champagne brunch for two on the terrace is a frequent delight. Shell-handled flatware and Japanese fans serving as placemats take part in the unpredictable mix.

ABOVE: In the library the antique daybed, covered in silk, and the mirrored wall figure prominently in the designer's solution for enlarging space. Cecil Beaton's sketch from Turandot peeks from behind another Kuan Yin.

RIGHT: The master bedroom is a highly personal statement. Photographs, books and papers are stacked up everywhere. Rustic ceiling beams slope toward an 18th-century screen with hand-tinted engravings. Antique velvet bed hangings and a Portuguese needlepoint rug enrich the warm, unorthodox mixture.

Michael Taylor

Michael Taylor

*"It's essential for me, not merely to
live with beautiful things, but to
perfect my own approach to interior
design. I wouldn't describe myself as
a collector so much as a student of
line, form and beauty."*

From almost every window, there is a view of the constant and ever-changing sea. High on a cliff near San Francisco's Presidio, the combined studio, office and home of interior designer Michael Taylor has a rare and poetic location. With the Pacific Ocean on the left and the Golden Gate Bridge on the right, the view is unparalleled—expansive and unpredictable.

Appropriately enough, *expansive* and *unpredictable* are words that might well be applied to Michael Taylor himself—to his personality, to his work and to his collections of art, antiques and natural objects. His collections considered as a whole are extravagantly diverse, ranging from Roman torsos to Jean-Michel Frank furniture; from Régence to contemporary; from ammonites of the Mesozoic era to Byzantine mosaics.

"I've acquired some of these things over a period of more than thirty years," says the designer. "I change them around often, and many move on to the people for whom I design—or I have copies made. Nothing is a prop, and nothing is here simply for effect or acquisition. I live with these beautiful things almost temporarily, and I regard myself as a custodian more than anything else. This is my design laboratory, if you will, a place where I can study forms and effects and combinations. That's the reason there are so many different styles and periods represented here; so much that is man-made, so much that is natural and organic. When I began my career, it was essential for a decorator to be familiar with every period and with every style, to satisfy all moods. My own approach is still flexible.

Not surprisingly, his own passion for collecting began early, at the age of eight, when he was bringing home living plants and unusual rocks, some of which he still has. By the age of ten he was already exploring antiques shops in expeditions undertaken with a favorite grandmother. As he grew older, it became almost inevitable that his career would lie in the decorative arts.

He soon settled into the field of interior design.

He owned a succession of showrooms and antiques shops, and before long his reputation and clientele were international. Many of the ideas of this California-born designer have been seminal. He was, for example, one of the first designers to bring plants indoors, to use slate floors extensively and to conceive of using large-scale furniture even in the smallest areas. Today, on projects that take him all over the United States and Europe, he is inclined to move in a contemporary direction.

"Basically I believe in the freedom of space," he explains. "And I've often recommended that the people for whom I design invest in contemporary art. The fact is that today, superior antiques are scarce, if not impossible to find, and they have become fantastically expensive. I'd far rather see the people I work for in an effective contemporary setting than surrounded by inferior antiques. I love beautiful things, but I hate pretension."

As a consequence, his own collections are remarkably out of the ordinary, selected with a careful eye for line and form and style. Given a choice, he prefers the unusual—indeed, the unique. Whenever possible, for example, he is inclined to choose Irish rather than English silver; Portuguese rather than Spanish furniture; a French-style period piece made in Denmark—everything the best of its kind.

This talent for innovation and reinterpretation and his ability to mix apparently irreconcilable styles are the hallmarks of Michael Taylor's talent. "It's simply that I like to take the unexpected course, to find a harmony not immediately obvious to the untrained eye," explains the designer.

With the sound of the ocean below and the view of ships passing in and out of San Francisco Harbor, the location of Michael Taylor's house and office symbolizes the eloquent way he continually succeeds in bringing together artifice and nature. Contrast exists, as well as a compelling unity. The living room itself—with its crystal chandeliers, its lacquer and gleaming French furniture, its plants and fragments of stone—is paradoxically attuned to the sea beyond. The same is true of the bedroom, where a splendid and elaborate four-poster bed is part of the beauty outside, only the thickness of glass away.

This harmony of house and sea appears most dramatically in Mr. Taylor's office. The area is far more contemporary in feeling than the rest of the interior, and it abounds with unexpected natural objects: huge Mexican geodes on the slate floor; the desk, a slab of antique French wood on stone pedestals; ammonites—the fossilized remains of giant snails, millions of years old—scattered here and there; a woven Philippine basket of enormous size; a number of plants; driftwood, rocks.

The house and its collections are in constant flux and movement, as is the sea below. The constant, however, is Michael Taylor's own vision and perception of relationships, his exact eye for the purity of line and proportion. "I really think it all came from my grandmother," he says. "When I was very young, she made me aware not only of furniture and antiques but of the beauty of nature itself. She taught me why we react to a fine line, whether in a piece of furniture or in a flower. I've never forgotten."

RIGHT: A striking arrangement of antiquities—some natural, others highly civilized—rests on the entrance hall's terra-cotta floor tiles. The natural formations are stone geodes; the marble torso, busts and capital fragment date from the Roman Empire.

"Nothing is a prop, and nothing is here simply for effect."

OPPOSITE: *The luxurious living room typifies the harmonious interplay of a wide range of civilizations and periods, textures and surfaces, which is characteristic of the design. The graceful lines of the Régence mantel are reiterated by a Louis XV bureau plat. Other appointments include a Louis XIV mirror, Jean-Michel Frank granite table, and Genoese crystal chandelier.*

ABOVE: *A country French iron and rock crystal chandelier and low antique vermeil candlesticks illuminate the many rich surfaces brought together in the dining room. A 15th-century Italian olive-wood credenza stretches beneath the 17th-century Roman overdoor panel, while ammonites and large Etruscan jars serve as adornments. Leather-upholstered Irish Louis XIII chairs surround the 19th-century English Regency-design table from Italy.*

ABOVE: *Fishtail palms and a Yosemite slate floor add organic life and natural shapes to the cosmopolitan tranquillity of the master bedroom. Clear ocean light washes over an arrangement of Etruscan and pre-Columbian artifacts on a thick rustic table, which is accompanied by a finely carved and gessoed Louis XV chair. The unusual wall brackets, English giltwood mirror and Italian commode are all 18th century.*

RIGHT: *Contrasting with an elaborately carved and gilded 17th-century Spanish bed is the rusticity of an 18th-century English twig-motif table. Above the Dutch commode are a Matisse drawing and an 18th-century still life.*

Credits and Acknowledgments

Photographers

Jaime Ardiles-Arce   28–33, 68–73, 148–153, 156–161,
   164–169, 180–185

Richard Champion   36–41, 76–81, 132–137

Angelo Donghia   84–89

Oberto Gili   188–193

Horst   124–129

Russell MacMasters   12–17, 44–49, 60–65, 92–97, 116–
   121, 132–137, 196–201, 204–209

Derry Moore   172–177

Mary Nichols   52–57

William Steele   108–113

Peter Vitale   18–25

Charles S. White   4–9, 100–105, 140–145

Designers' portraits by:

Cris Alexander   155

Blackstone-Shelburne   34

Jim Britt   130

Richard Champion   74

Arthur Coleman Photography©   50

Kenn Duncan   82

John Engstead   194

Feliciano   18, 66, 122, 170

John Haynsworth   162

Christophe von Hohenberg   178

David Keller   110

Hubert Latimer   2

Bob Lukeman   162

Russell MacMasters   58, 90, 114, 202

J. Reid   186

Mathew Rolston   146

Steve Shadley   26

©Skrebneski   98

Philip Turner Photography   42

Donald Wristen   138

Andrew R. Zawrocki   106

Writers

The following writers prepared the original *Architectural
Digest* articles from which the material in this book has
been adapted:

Peter Carlsen   Valentine Lawford

Kay Crosby Ellis   Lars Lerup

Lois Wagner Green   John Loring

John Gruen   Cameron Curtis McKinley

Timothy Hawkins   Suzanne Stark Morrow

Richard Horn   Wendy Murphy

Frank Israel   Carolyn Noren

All original text and captions adapted by Joanne Jaffe
Introduction by Russell Lynes
Special thanks to Margaret Redfield, Sylvia Tidwell and
Lyle Bayle

Design

Book design, page layout and mechanics by
   Mike Yazzolino

Jacket design by Charles Ross

The Knapp Press
is a wholly owned subsidary of
KNAPP COMMUNICATIONS CORPORATION.
Chairman and Chief Executive Officer:
   Cleon T. Knapp
President: H. Stephen Cranston
Senior Vice-Presidents:
   Rosalie Bruno (*New Venture
      Development*)
   Betsy Wood Knapp (*MIS Electronic
      Media*)
   Harry Myers (*Magazine Group
      Publisher*)
   William J. N. Porter (*Corporate
      Product Sales*)
   Paige Rense (*Editorial*)
   L. James Wade, Jr. (*Finance*)

THE KNAPP PRESS

President: Alice Bandy; Administrative Assistant: Beth Bell;
Editor: Norman Kolpas; Managing Editor: Pamela Mosher;
Associate Editors: Jan Koot, Sarah Lifton, Diane Rossen
Worthington; Assistant Editors: Colleen Dunn Bates, Nancy
D. Roberts; Editorial Assistant: Teresa Roupe; Art Director:
Paula Schlosser; Designer: Robin Murawski; Book
Production Manager: Larry Cooke; Book Production
Coordinators: Veronica Losorelli, Joan Valentine; Director,

Rosebud Books: Robert Groag: Creative Director, Rosebud
Books: Jeff Book; Financial Manager: Joseph Goodman;
Assistant Finance Manager: Kerri Culbertson; Financial
Assistant: Julie Mason; Fulfillment Services Manager:
Virginia Parry; Director of Public Relations: Jan B. Fox;
Marketing Assistants: Dolores Briqueleur, Randy Levin;
Promotions Managers: Joanne Denison, Nina Gerwin;
Special Sales Manager: Lynn Blocker; Special Sales
Coordinator: Amy Hershman

We would also like to acknowledge Patrick R. Casey, Vice-
President, Production, Knapp Communications
Corporation; Anthony P. Iacono, Vice-President,
Manufacturing, Knapp Communications Corporation;
Philip Kaplan, Vice-President, Graphics, Knapp
Communications Corporation; Donna Clipperton, Dean
Larrabee and Faith Haase, Rights and Permissions, Knapp
Communications Corporation.

This book is set in Zapf International
Composition was on the Merganthaler Linotron 202 by
   Graphic Typesetting Service
Text stock: 100 lb. Northcote Web Gloss, furnished by
   WWF Paper Corporation West
Color separation and film work by
   Liberty Photo Engraving Company
Printing and binding by Kingsport Press